Wicked
Shreveport

Wicked
Shreveport

Bernadette J. Palombo, Gary D. Joiner,
W. Chris Hale and Cheryl H. White

Published by The History Press
Charleston, SC 29403
www.historypress.net

Copyright © 2012 by Bernadette J. Palombo, Gary D. Joiner,
W. Chris Hale and Cheryl H. White

All rights reserved

First published 2012

Manufactured in the United States

ISBN 978.1.59629.818.7

Library of Congress Cataloging-in-Publication Data

Wicked Shreveport / Bernadette J. Palombo ... [et al.].
p. cm.
Includes bibliographical references.
ISBN 978-1-59629-818-7
1. Crime--Louisiana--Shreveport--History. 2. Crime--Louisiana--Shreveport Region-
-History. 3. Corruption--Louisiana--Shreveport--History. 4. Scandals--Louisiana--
Shreveport--History. 5. Criminals--Louisiana--Shreveport--Biography. 6. Shreveport
(La.)--Social conditions. 7. Shreveport (La.)--History. 8. Shreveport (La.)--Biography. I.
Palombo, Bernadette Jones.
HV6795.S527W53 2012
364.109763'99--dc23
2011052414

Notice: The information in this book is true and complete to the best of our knowledge. It is offered without guarantee on the part of the author or The History Press. The author and The History Press disclaim all liability in connection with the use of this book.

All rights reserved. No part of this book may be reproduced or transmitted in any form whatsoever without prior written permission from the publisher except in the case of brief quotations embodied in critical articles and reviews.

Contents

Acknowledgements	7
1. Frontier Violence: Vengeance Is Mine	9
2. Lynching: The Hard Hand of Swift Justice	21
3. The Ku Klux Klan in Northwest Louisiana	33
4. Blind Tigers and Bootlegging in Caddo Parish During Prohibition	47
5. The Red-Light District in Shreveport	59
6. The Butterfly Man: The Last Murderer Hanged in Shreveport, Louisiana	71
7. Crime of the Great Depression: The Era of Bonnie and Clyde	85
8. Serial Killers: Rolling and Code	95
Notes	105
Bibliography	119
About the Authors	127

Acknowledgements

We wish to acknowledge the assistance of Dominica Carriere and Shawn Bohannon, curators at the Louisiana State University in Shreveport, Archives and Special Collections. Their expertise is unequalled. Joe Slattery, research librarian at Shreve Memorial Library, Broadmoor Branch provided valuable insight.

We also want to thank local historians Eric Brock, Clifton Cardin, John Andrew Prime and Mary Margaret Richard. They have been good friends and possess a vast array of knowledge on the history of our region.

Finally, during the course of writing this book, some of our students helped share the burdens of research. They made our tasks much easier. We will always be grateful to Sara Carpenter, Blake Lee, Laulie Pasquier, Elisha Scott and Laura Beeman.

1
Frontier Violence: Vengeance Is Mine

Gary D. Joiner, PhD

In those days a man who shot to kill was not necessarily a bad man.
—Albert Harris Leonard

The history of the western frontier is the story of the civilization of a great untamed wilderness. The rules of law and order, with their intricacies of due process, were often nonexistent, ignored or loosely followed. Particularly in the Deep South and the rapidly expanding West, the majority of townsmen and rural landowners approved of and encouraged swift social justice for heinous crimes. Most people believed that due process was an inexact science at best and sometimes a travesty. The concept of social justice in these regions began with the English colonies and can be traced to older European roots. If the public believed someone was guilty, it wanted punishment immediately because it did not trust courts to deliver swift or fair justice.[1]

Shreveport, Louisiana, is typical of frontier towns. Although it may be difficult today to identify Louisiana's third-largest city with the great westward migration, it was once on the edge of the West. Located on the Red River near the northwestern corner of the state, Shreveport's strategic location prepared it for growth. Rising above the river on a one-square-mile plateau, the original town site was not prone to flooding. Some twenty miles to the west lay Texas and thirty miles to the north, Arkansas. When incorporated in 1839, Shreveport was, for a short period, the westernmost municipality in the United States. Four years prior to this, the settlement began as Shreve Town. The prospects for the young village appeared bright, except for one enormous problem. For over one hundred miles above and for a short distance below the site, the river was clogged with a massive logjam. Some settlers lived along the banks of the river, but commerce by riverboat was impossible.

Captain Henry Miller Shreve was awarded a contract by the U.S. Army to clear the "Great Raft," as it was known. He began working on the river in the early 1830s and continued throughout the decade. Shreve accomplished this task by bringing in Irish immigrants and slave labor, who used specialized vessels called snagboats. He plugged up side streams, made shortcuts called cutoffs and generally rerouted the river whenever it suited him. While working on the raft, Shreve and his business partners engineered a treaty with the Caddo Indians in 1835, effectively removing them from the region. He also laid out the streets of the new town, which formed the grid for downtown Shreveport. The massacres at Goliad and the Alamo were still hot topics, and Shreve paid homage to the fallen heroes, naming Crockett, Fannin, Milam and Travis Streets for their leaders. Caddo Street, Louisiana Avenue and Texas Street all reflected the region as well.

With the river open, steamboats began their passages up the still dangerous river. Unseen snags often ripped open the hulls of the boats. Boiler explosions were a frequent source of steamboat losses as well. The steamboat captains on the sketchily charted western rivers often manned their vessels with immigrants and others who learned their jobs while aboard the boats. Sometimes these men would settle in or near one of the new ports of call, wishing to adopt a calmer lifestyle. The original Indian paths to the west became the Texas Trail, along which cattle herds moved east for transport on the river to market. Even during and after the Civil War, Shreveport was a major port for the cattle trade.[2] Settlers arrived by steamboat or, less frequently, overland from eastern Louisiana via the Monroe Road. Shreveport readily accepted these new settlers. Many of the town's early citizens came from faraway places like Pomerania, Lithuania, Russian Poland, Alsace and Prussia.[3] Jews, Catholics and Protestants all made their way to the new town, seeking a better life. Some came as merchants and others as laborers. Together with the existing Anglo community, they forged the new community into a budding commercial center.

Regional commerce began almost immediately. The river trade fed immigration. Huge areas of flat fertile land along the river were opened for

Frontier Violence: Vengeance Is Mine

cotton planting. Prior to the Civil War, the plantations required slave labor to clear the land and plant and harvest the "white gold" (cotton). After the war, sharecroppers performed the work. Usually, these were the same people.

Cattlemen, planters, riverboat men, farm workers, residents of the town, soldiers and, later, railroad workers all sought entertainment, which included prostitution and gambling, as well as more genteel pursuits. Often, competing interests and desires led to disputes, making violence common. Shootings and stabbings were frequently the result. A band of about one hundred heavily armed Texans briefly seized Shreveport in 1839 before the villagers gathered their allies from the surrounding area and drove them out. The apparent intent of the raid was to annex the river port into the Republic of Texas.[4]

The earliest chronicler of life in Shreveport was Albert Harris Leonard. Born in Columbus, Georgia, in 1839, Leonard's father moved the family to Shreveport in October 1849.[5] At that time, Shreveport's stores and homes hugged the Red River and Cross Bayou, which flowed into the river on the north side of the plateau. The following year, the 1850 census reported that the population of Caddo Parish was 8,884, with 2,130 being free and 5,208 slaves. The census also reported a total of 747 families in the parish. Shreveport's population was 1,163.[6]

Leonard recounts several violent incidents, beginning soon after his arrival in Shreveport. He reported that a man walked into a doctor's office and started a gunfight in which both men were killed. The doctor was William Mercer Green, and the instigator was an acting state legislator named David Hester.[7] Three months later, the ten-year-old boy watched from his room as a man ran out of the Catfish Hotel closely pursued by a second man wielding a Bowie knife. The second man killed the first before Leonard's eyes.[8] Among young Albert's new friends was Rufus "Rufe" Sewall. Rufe's father, Rufus Sewall Sr., was gunned down in a duel with Dr. Joel Hardwick. The duel was fought at the intersection of Texas Street and Spring Street. Hardwick was acquitted in the death.[9] The elder Sewall's brother, John Octavius Sewall, was Shreveport's first mayor. While in office, he was killed in a duel by John Willson. The encounter took place on January 6, 1840, across the line in Elysian Fields, Texas, supposedly over a liquor ordinance but probably over an affair with Willson's wife.[10] Sometimes, a man confronted his enemy in an unorthodox manner and got away with it. Leonard recounts being an eyewitness to a killing in which Dr. William Head dispatched a bully named

James Patteson Flournoy Sr. *From* History of Shreveport and Shreveport Builders, *292.*

Bill Oliver. He walked across Texas Street into a saloon, immediately firing at the unsuspecting man and killing him instantly. Dr. Head was brought before a magistrate, who discharged him because Oliver had bullied him.[11]

James Patteson Flournoy Sr., widely known as "J. Pat," was born in Pulaski, Tennessee, in 1853. His family moved to Caddo Parish shortly afterward. They settled one mile east of the town of Greenwood to be with other family members, including J. Pat's grandfather Alfred Flournoy. The families were wealthy planters and influential politically. J. Pat later became one of the most important sheriffs in Caddo Parish.[12]

In his memoirs, Flournoy observed that "in those days if a man spoke ill of any lady, it cost him his life."[13] He remembered this in 1860, as the Vicksburg, Shreveport & Texas Railroad was under construction in Caddo Parish.[14] The chief engineer was a Colonel Word. The second senior man was Captain Orr. Word roomed at the Garrett Hotel in Greenwood, owned by Flournoy's father, Alonzo Flournoy. Word was seeing a young lady named Sue Head. Orr attempted to date Sue's sister. The girls' father was Dr. William Head, who also had two sons. Dr. Head was very close to his daughters and "extremely careful" about the people with whom they socialized. Dr. Head sought information about Colonel Word from a source in Alabama. The source discovered that both Colonel Word and Captain Orr were married but that they had filed for divorce. This was not good enough for Dr. Head, who confronted the railroad men and told them he would kill both if they tried to see his daughters again. Dr. Head went on a business trip and, returning home, found Word in his parlor with his daughter Sue. Dr. Head shot the man, who died later in his room at the Garrett Hotel. Three weeks later, Head found Orr in his rooming house and also killed him. Dr. Head then had his black houseman dump Orr's body in the back of the garden in a patch of oats, an action that residents of Greenwood considered excessive.

Dr. Head left for Shreveport. While he was gone, one of his sons, sixteen-year-old Charley, and a friend went duck hunting and were confronted by a sheriff's posse who believed Charley was the murderer. One of the posse members was Charley's friend Tom Adams. The two got into a fight during the arrest, and Charley threatened to kill Tom. Needless to say, the boys' friendship waned, and shortly afterward, Dr. Head and Charley armed themselves and went to the Adams Farm to kill Tom. As the pair approached, Tom got his gun and escaped through a trapdoor under the house. He then went into Greenwood, where he bought another gun and a horse. Tom lay in ambush for Dr. Head, who was traveling with Charley in a buggy. As the father and son neared the first store in Greenwood, Tom stepped out of the bushes and killed Dr. Head instantly with blasts from a double-barreled shotgun. Charley returned fire but missed. Tom then killed Charley with twin blasts from the second gun, mounted his horse and left for Texas, never to return.[15]

From the beginning, Shreveport and the surrounding regions struggled over their future. They could choose from two possible directions: "The Spirit of the Frontier" (vigilante justice) or the "Civilization of the South" (due process).[16] Both described solutions to immediate problems. The former promised immediate gratification and retribution. The latter promised the rule of law and opportunity for growth. Stability was thrust upon Shreveport following secession and the beginning of the Civil War. After the fall of New Orleans, Shreveport became a major transshipment point by forwarding cattle and supplies from Texas east to Confederate armies across the Mississippi River. Beginning in March 1863, Shreveport became not only the largest Confederate-held city in Louisiana but also the military headquarters of the Army of the Trans-Mississippi and the Confederate

William Clarke Quantrill. *State Historical Society of Missouri, Columbia.*

capital of the state. Refugees flooded in from southern Louisiana. Some stayed in northwest Louisiana, while others moved on to East Texas. Thousands of troops were stationed in and around the city. Most came from Louisiana, Texas, Arkansas and Missouri. Some became unwanted visitors.

Among the most infamous of guerilla fighters in the West during the Civil War was Confederate colonel William Clarke Quantrill. His best-known raid was against Lawrence, Kansas, on August 21, 1863, during which Quantrill's raiders burned the homes and businesses of people he suspected of carrying Unionist destruction in Missouri.[17] The devastation was so widespread and the viciousness so thorough that Quantrill's superiors wanted him sacked or killed. Quantrill was ordered to the military headquarters in Shreveport to personally explain his actions to the department commander, Lieutenant General Edmund Kirby Smith.[18] Smith seemed to like the audacious cavalryman, and the meetings went well until Sunday, November 22, 1863. On that morning, Reverend George Tucker, the pastor of First Baptist Church of Shreveport, had delivered his sermon to the congregation and was preaching at another service for blacks. One of Quantrill's captains rode his horse into the church and insulted Tucker's wife, Abigail. Reverend Tucker pulled out a pistol and killed the offending cavalryman.[19] Life continued

Frontier Violence: Vengeance Is Mine

in some form of normalcy through the remainder of the Civil War.

When Union occupying forces entered Shreveport in early June 1865, the city and the state of Louisiana came under the same rule of martial law that New Orleans had seen since May 1862. The Federal army established a headquarters in Shreveport, and from there, life entered into a new phase—one of military rule. Louisianians began the long, painful process of finding out which groups had rights and which did not. The era of Reconstruction had begun.

Former Confederate officers and soldiers believed they should continue to have a voice in local and regional political affairs. Republicans, the victorious party of Lincoln, composed of both white and black veterans, politicians and entrepreneurs, attempted to control the legislature and the government as a whole. The number of freed slaves exceeded the white population in the state, and this segment of society was a natural recruiting ground for the Republicans.[20] A large street battle was fought in New Orleans in 1866, so widely reported and violent that Congress established the Military Reconstruction Act on March 2, 1867. This became the standard model for what has been often labeled Radical Reconstruction of the South.

Reverend George Tucker. *Collection of Eric J. Brock.*

Shreveport, the last state capital of the Confederacy to fall, untouched by the ravages of war and a large center of population and wealth, became a focal point of resistance. The U.S. Army and the Republican Party expanded the voter rolls with blacks and some white residents. Governor James Madison Wells and the legislature called for a new constitution to replace an ill-advised document created under the Union army's direction in 1864. The vote was to take place in 1868. White ex-Confederates and former politicians operated under a variety of secret society names and attempted to work against the new order's attempt at domination.

Potential black voters were harassed, threatened and beaten, and many were killed to force the point. Caddo, Bossier and St. Landry parishes witnessed the worst violence. So thorough was the intimidation that in the presidential election that fall, only one of the 2,987 registered Republicans in Caddo Parish voted for U.S. Grant, the Republican nominee.[21] The month before, in October, the vote for the state constitution had brought massive political violence in northwest Louisiana. Forty-two people in Caddo Parish were murdered for being registered Republicans. At the same time in Bossier Parish, 172 were assassinated for the same reason.[22] The Constitution of 1868 passed, but the political violence did not wane. The federal troops controlled the cities and towns during the day, but the nightriders controlled the roads at night. The U.S. Army simply could not be everywhere at all times. What the ex-Confederates and their allies could not do, nature helped accomplish as the people of northern Louisiana regained home rule in 1873.

Shreveport and the surrounding region suffered greatly in the most severe threat to its existence. In the late summer and fall of 1873, a devastating yellow fever epidemic struck with such force that approximately one-quarter of the population of those remaining in the town in late August were dead from the disease by early November. Of approximately 4,000 people who remained in the city, 816 were buried, mostly in mass graves, in Oakland Cemetery.[23] An additional 41 people were known dead in the immediate vicinity of Shreveport, and a priest and 4 nuns were buried at St. Vincent's Convent cemetery.[24] The "List of the Dead" reveals one victim who did not succumb to the dreaded "Yellow Jack." Instead, he died from a gunshot.

Many people who could fled the stricken city early before a quarantine was established. Among those was Leopold Baer, a merchant who owned a grocery store on Texas Street. Baer moved to Marshall, Texas, not knowing that he carried the fever with him. He left his store in the hands of a night watchman named Glass. As the fever strangled Shreveport, a gang of burglars broke into empty storefronts to steal what they could. Sometime during Monday night, September 30, a group attempted to break into Baer's store. Sitting in the dark with a .32-caliber pistol was the night watchman, Glass. As the door was pried open, Glass fired the pistol and killed C.E. Pritchard, a twenty-eight-year-old opportunistic hoodlum. Glass was immediately cleared of the killing, and Pritchard's body was thrown into the yellow fever mound in Oakland Cemetery with no fanfare.[25] Leopold Baer died of yellow fever in Marshall a week later, on September 8. His body was later returned to Shreveport, and he was buried in Hebrew Rest within Oakland Cemetery.[26]

Frontier Violence: Vengeance Is Mine

The U.S. Army was forced to retreat from the Red River and Ouachita River Valleys, fearing for their own safety. While Reconstruction technically ended in the state with the presidential election of 1877, it effectively ended in north Louisiana in 1873. A massacre occurred in Colfax in Grant Parish in April. Yellow fever ended occupation that fall. Indicative of the political tone of that time was a front-page story in the *Shreveport Times* of July 9, 1874. The publisher was Albert Harris Leonard. Describing a series of resolutions in the town of Greenwood concerning "Carpet-baggers and Negroes," Leonard wrote:

> *The riddance of Louisiana of the presence of carpet-baggers and scallawags* [sic] *is in reality the grand idea of this rallying of white people of the State. While we propose to elect only educated, capable and honest white men to office, we do not propose to deprive the negro of his rights; indeed, in protecting ourselves in our rights, we shall protect him in his. We are not warring upon the negro,* but we are warring to the death upon carpet-baggers and scallawags *just as we are warring upon thieves, murderers, perjurers, and all infamous characters. Hereafter in all our resolutions, it seems to us, it would be well to make these distinctions prominent and clear.*[27]

Leonard received his wish. With Reconstruction policies found to be political and economic disasters, Congress grew tired of funding the occupation troops. Louisiana and the South returned to home rule under archconservatives, known in Louisiana as the Bourbons. Life reached normalcy under a very lax central government. Each parish was allowed to handle its own affairs, and little was done to interfere with politics under the rule of Jim Crow. In Shreveport, as in other cities across the South, most people focused their activities on pursuits other than politics.

Gambling as a recreational vice was part of life in Shreveport from the beginning. Throughout the nineteenth century, saloons and private venues offered games of skill and chance almost nonstop. An all-night card game was played in a two-story brick store at the northwest corner of Common Street and Milam Street in Shreveport, ending on Sunday morning, June 14, 1885. Among the card players was Gus Logan, a black man with an unsavory reputation as a gambler and a petty criminal.[28] Another player was Nathan Goldkind, a native of Plotsk, in Russian Poland.[29] Goldkind was thirty-six years old, single, a storeowner and an avid gambler. While gambling was his

Nathan Goldkind's store at the corner of Common Street and Milam Street, taken in 1985. *Photography by Eric J. Brock.*

passion, it would also be his undoing. Goldkind carried scars from stabbings, including a slit throat, and was missing his left middle finger, blown off his hand in a shooting.[30] Logan could not determine whether Goldkind was a skilled gambler or a cheater. He grabbed Goldkind's own pistol and fired a round through the unfortunate man's left eye. Goldkind dropped to the floor, dead before he landed. Logan ran across the street and was immediately arrested and taken to jail to await trial. During the trial, one of the other gamblers testified that Logan said, "Damn if he ain't dead" before he dropped the pistol used in the murder. In short order, Logan was found guilty of murder and sentenced to be hanged by a Caddo district judge. The sentence was appealed, and the case moved rapidly up the judicial ladder to the Louisiana Supreme Court.[31]

Logan, found guilty of murder, was to be hanged. However, Governor Samuel Douglas McEnery decided otherwise and commuted the sentence to life at hard labor, not an unusual action for the governor.[32] Four years later, Logan was free, and the Jewish community was outraged. Goldkind's friend,

Frontier Violence: Vengeance Is Mine

White bronze monument of Nathan Goldkind, Oakland Cemetery, Shreveport, Louisiana. *Photography by Gary D. Joiner.*

Louis Liebman, placed a "white bronze" or zinc monument at his grave facing Baker Street in Oakland Cemetery. Passersby can read: "Nathan Goldkind. A Native of Plotsk, Russian Poland. Killed in Shreveport, Louisiana, by Gus Logan, June 14, 1885, Aged 36 Years." Below this, in large capital letters, are the words: "IN GOD HE TRUSTED."

2
Lynching: The Hard Hand of Swift Justice

Gary D. Joiner, PhD

A Straw in the Restless Wind.
—Shreveport Journal

Violence has always been a part of American history. As westward migration spread across the continent, the rule of law often lagged behind. Popular culture is filled with images of gunfights, bank robberies and bands of marauders burning and looting the homes of innocent families. Another common scene is of a lone lawman holding off an angry mob, with simple townsmen wanting vengeance for a horrific crime, their intent to hang the scoundrel before he could be tried. The reality of these scenes is closer to the truth than most might believe. Even in areas where courts and a sound legal system were firmly in place, the popular concepts of how justice should be meted out competed with due process.

The death penalty, still a hot topic today, has played a central role in the judicial system. During most of American history, the questions about the death penalty centered not on whether someone should be executed but on how and by whom. All across the United States, except in New England, swift executions by mobs of citizens were at times more prevalent than court-ordered sentences of death. If the execution occurred outside of legal proceedings, it was usually called a lynching. The term comes from a justice of the peace, Charles Lynch, who informally ordered the death of Loyalists during the American Revolution. From the 1800s through the years following World War II, lynchings were usually carried out by hanging, but victims were also tied up and shot, burned at the stake or mutilated. The bodies were left hanging for all to see.

The South and West accounted for most of these informal killings. In the West, the deaths were frequently associated with "vigilance committees" whose members were called "vigilantes." A person could be hanged for almost any reason the members believed to be acceptable, from petty theft and horse stealing to murder and rape. Race was rarely an issue. The South posed a different set of circumstances, and historians have treated it separately. The overwhelming majority of lynchings in the South were conducted by white mobs executing black men. Sometimes women were lynched, and there are cases, even in northern Louisiana, of black mobs lynching blacks.

Southern lynchings have such a complex background that scholars have divided the practice into types based on how the event was carried out. The first, and perhaps best, study of southern lynchings was undertaken by the Tuskegee Institute in Alabama in 1940. By 1959, the Tuskegee study had amassed a list of 4,733 lynchings in the United States between 1882 and 1959.[33] The study defined a lynching as a killing that meets certain criteria: "there must be legal evidence that a person has been killed, and that he met his death illegally at the hands of a group [meaning at least three people] acting under the pretext of service to justice, race, or tradition."[34]

Aside from determining whether someone was lynched or legally executed, another major objective was to identify what kind of group performed the act. Most scholars use criteria developed by Fitzhugh Brundage, who categorized lynching groups by size and purpose. Mass lynching mobs involved large numbers of people who came together informally and approved of the act. Private lynchings were conducted by small groups that acted on vengeance, typically to avenge a wrong done to a relative. Terrorist mobs were organized—long-lasting groups that used lynching and intimidation for economic or political purposes. This is best typified by the Ku Klux Klan. Another group that lynched, either with legal permission or without it, was the posse. Posses were groups of men who were sworn in as a type of militia to assist with law enforcement. They were usually gathered to track down suspects of crimes or escapees.[35] They were sometimes uniformed and were similar to vigilantes. All of these forms of frontier justice evolved quickly into mature forms after the Civil War.

Lynching: The Hard Hand of Swift Justice

Prior to the Civil War, slaves were kept on plantations by roving groups of nightriders who patrolled the rural roads. If slaves were caught away from their plantation without a pass from the owner, usually a metal or wooden token called a slave tag, or a written permission slip, they were returned. It was up to the slave owner to determine punishment. During the Civil War, this function was sometimes taken over by the military, but slave owners still retained decisions regarding punishment unless the slave was leased to the Confederate government for construction projects. After the war, with the slaves freed, southern society faced huge issues.

The federal government had no clear plan for the former slaves. White society wanted the old system to continue, but without slavery. The U.S. Army remained in the South to keep the peace and control the southern states. The former slaves were illiterate because it had been illegal to teach them to read and write. Now, with freedom in hand, many demanded an elevated place in society. Following a large race riot in New Orleans in 1866, Congress passed the Military Reconstruction Act, and Louisiana and the other southern states went under martial law. Shreveport became a large headquarters for the military, and companies of cavalry were stationed in the larger towns. They patrolled the roads and kept the peace. Their actions were harsh, particularly when dealing with the former Confederate soldiers. In 1873, the tide turned. Yellow fever broke out in Shreveport, and the military units evacuated. Home rule returned in northwest Louisiana, and four years later, Reconstruction ended.

The harsh memories of Reconstruction reinforced white democratic politicians' plans to regain and keep control. Intimidation of blacks was designed to keep them under control, and lynching was a means to accomplish that. The newspapers of the day accepted this idea of rough justice as a proper tool. Law enforcement and the courts often concurred.[36] Some parishes were more enthusiastic about lynching than others. Lynchings were frequent in the Florida parishes and the lower Mississippi River parishes, but northern Louisiana saw the largest numbers of lynchings.[37] Between 1874 and 1946, 421 lynchings were recorded in Louisiana, and of these, 78 were recorded in Caddo, Bossier, DeSoto and Webster Parishes.[38] During this period, the three parishes with the most lynchings were Bossier Parish, 36; Ouachita Parish, 32; and Caddo Parish, 26.

Several authors believe that lynchings in the South were almost completely driven by racial hatred or the need, at whatever cost, to maintain economic

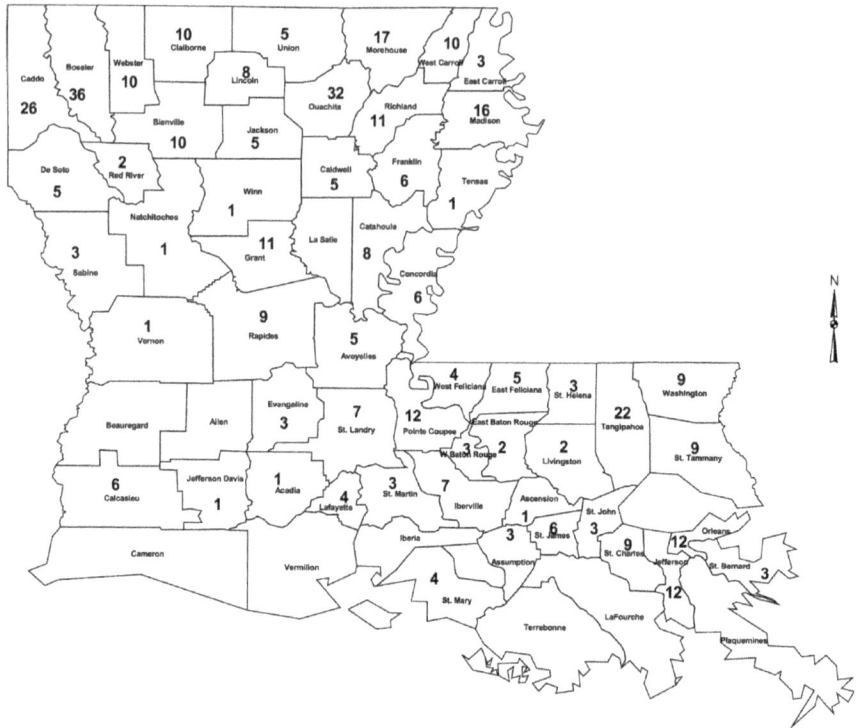

Map of Louisiana showing the number of lynchings by parish between 1874 and 1946. *Cartography by Gary D. Joiner.*

control over blacks.[39] Newspaper editorial writers in the upper Midwest and New England tended to share this view, particularly if the paper was black owned. Before 1900, their counterparts in the South most often viewed lynchings as a proper form of swift justice, focusing on the cause rather than the result. After 1900, with a renewed growth in cities and the middle class, lynching was more likely to be looked upon as an outmoded form of justice that should be replaced by due process in the courts.[40]

The evolution to a more equitable form of justice took decades. The people who often took to the streets and roads of the area looking for violent criminals had to be educated. Posses or mobs, sometimes operating at the same time, raced to capture someone who was believed to have committed a vile crime. Confrontations between competing groups could be violent as well. Lynching as a result of violent crimes made up 63 of the 78 incidents in northwestern Louisiana. Lynchings in these parishes mirror the rest of

Lynching: The Hard Hand of Swift Justice

the state, but with more incidents, and can be best studied by reviewing the reasons for the acts and whether they occurred prior to or after 1901.

TABLE 1. LYNCHINGS IN BOSSIER, CADDO, DESOTO AND WEBSTER PARISHES BETWEEN 1881 AND 1946[41]
Spelling and wording comes directly from the original data gathered.

Reason for Lynching	1881–1900	1900–1946	Total
Murder or Attempted Murder	14	16	30
Murderous Assault	5	8	13
Rape or Attempted Rape	3	9	12
Conspiracy to Commit Murder	4	1	4
Arson (as a lone act)	3	1	4
Miscegenation*	1	3	5
Insulted White Woman	1	1	2
Stock Theft	2	0	2
Voodooism	1	0	1
Outrageous Act	1	0	1
Robbery (as a lone act)	0	1	1
Burglary (as a lone act)	1	0	1
Hung for his Land	0	1	1
Desperate Negro Gambler	0	1	1
TOTAL	36	42	78

*Miscegenation is defined as the mixing of races through marriage, cohabitation or sexual relations.

The common distrust of the legal system prior to the end of Reconstruction was firmly rooted in the manner by which legal proceedings were conducted by military or military-backed courts. Following the end of Reconstruction and the protection provided by the U.S. Army, local courts and law enforcement officers were forced to struggle to regain respect. Lynch mobs firmly believed that in dispensing harsh justice, they taught an important lesson that deterred inappropriate behavior. It also taught the assumed guilty party an irrevocably harsh lesson.

The sight of a lynched body hanging from a tree left indelible memories on those who saw it. Either in late 1876 or early 1877, attorney John Bernard

Slattery brought his new bride, Mary Frances, back to Shreveport from Omaha, Nebraska. As they made their way down Texas Street, they saw a man hanging from a tree on the courthouse square. The new Mrs. Slattery told her husband that she did not want to live in Shreveport and wanted to go back to Nebraska.[42] Despite the introduction to Shreveport, they stayed in town and raised their family there.

Lynchings were casually reported in newspapers, regardless of their political leanings. A report in the *Shreveport Times* on November 29, 1892, described a case in Caddo Parish. A black man named Nathan Andrews attempted to shoot his white landlord, W.F. Driscoll, who was evicting him. Andrews fired but missed. He then ran away and crossed the Red River into Bossier Parish, where a group of people chased him down. The *Times* then stated, "He was captured this afternoon and—well, Judge Lynch evidently presided over the court, as later advices [*sic*] say that he was found attached to a tree, about three miles from this city [Shreveport], on the Bossier side."[43]

In 1903, Jennie Steers, a black domestic servant working at the Beard Plantation in Caddo Parish, was accused of poisoning the lemonade of sixteen-year-old Elizabeth Dolan. Dolan, the daughter of Steers's employer, died. A mob took Jennie to a tree and, while demanding a confession, placed a noose around her neck and then hanged her.[44]

Lynch mobs sometimes reacted to court proceedings, exacting revenge for a legal outcome with which they did not agree. On April 9, 1912, Tom Miles, a twenty-nine-year-old black man, was acquitted of writing insulting notes to a white girl who worked in a downtown Shreveport department store. The police court indicated a lack of evidence.[45] The following day, after Miles was released from court, he was hanged from a tree in the city and his body was riddled with bullets.[46]

Some regional crimes made national news and were reported as the events unfolded. The first major crime of the twentieth century in northwest Louisiana made headlines from coast to coast. In 1901, John Gray Foster, a member of the most powerful family in North Louisiana, was twenty-three years old, single, educated at the University of Virginia and immensely wealthy.[47] His family owned huge cotton plantations on both sides of the Red River. His father, James Martin Foster Sr., the man who created much of the family's wealth, had died the previous December.[48] Anchoring the holdings on the west side of the river was Little Egypt Plantation. On the east side, the Foster Plantation originally contained

Lynching: The Hard Hand of Swift Justice

John Gray Foster from his memorial volume. *Collection of Mary T. McGuire.*

some 12,000 acres.[49] At the time of James Martin Foster Sr.'s death, the Bossier plantation contained about 7,220 acres.[50] John Gray Foster's sister, Alethea Lucille Foster, was married to Benton McMillin, the governor of Tennessee. His cousin, Murphy J. Foster, the previous governor of the state of Louisiana, had recently been elected a U.S. senator. That left John Gray Foster and his brothers to carry on the family empire. The Bossier Plantation was the scene of long-standing disputes between the workers and overseers.[51] On Wednesday, June 12, Foster was asked to come to the plantation and mediate.

Early that morning, the overseer, a man named Vickers, had trouble with a black worker who drew a pistol but did not fire. Initial reports stated that Foster arrived and reprimanded the worker, who in turn hit Foster on the head with a hoe. Foster returned to the plantation office and asked his doctor to determine whether he was badly injured.[52] Just before noon, Foster, accompanied by Vickers and another man, arrived at the worker's cabin to fire him. As he rode to the door of the cabin, the worker opened the door and fired at Foster twice with a shotgun, hitting him in the chest. The worker ran away as Foster's two companions found a buggy and took their wounded companion to the company store. He died just as they reached the store.[53]

The alarm was given on both sides of the river to track down the murderer. Hundreds of men armed themselves and sealed off the bridges and roads on both sides of the Red River. Foster's mother and his brother, James Martin Foster Jr., went to the plantation and took the body back to Shreveport. The twin scenes of frenetic activity and solemn mourning would mark the next week in northwest Louisiana. Outrage and anger mounted quickly as the manhunt for the villain spread. Sheriffs' posses in Caddo and Bossier parishes scoured the region. The perpetrator was identified as a man known as Prince Edwards. He was supposedly seen heading north on the Caddo side of the river near the town of Gilliam, and an armed posse and bloodhounds moved north to follow.[54] Hundreds of men came in from the surrounding region to find the man. It was soon learned that seventeen blacks had made their way, or were told to go, from the plantation to the nearby Kinnebrew Store.[55] It was believed that Edwards might be in there. A mob surrounded the store, and it appeared that the angry crowd would storm it and lynch all inside. Ostensibly, the sheriff was their protector, but in reality, the mob was in control. Both women and men were in the store.[56]

Word quickly spread that the assassin and the people inside the store were members of a conspiracy to kill Foster and Chief of Police Lake of Shreveport. The group in the store was led by a preacher named Frank Smith, who called himself "Prophet."[57] The male members of the church were each called "Prince." The self-termed "Church of God" was an apocalyptic group from Texas. The mob's tone turned uglier by the hour.

Events stabilized on Friday, June 14, as Shreveport prepared for the late afternoon funeral of John Gray Foster at First Presbyterian Church. Every business in town closed. Crowds lined Milam Street to see the cortege. The ministers of the largest churches in Shreveport all eulogized the fallen planter.[58] A quartet composed of a future governor, the wife of the district attorney of Caddo Parish, the wife of a prominent attorney and a major land developer sang hymns.[59]

People from across the region wanted revenge. Sheriff Alexander Rodgers Thompson of Bossier Parish talked the mob into allowing him to move the prisoners to the Benton jail, and they agreed. Prince Edwards was not found with the group. The two most prominent members of the group were their leader, Prophet Smith, and F.D. McLand. Governor William Wright Heard told the sheriff not to let the mob have the prisoners. On June 15, the mob moved to Benton and surrounded the jail. While all these events unfolded, the telegraph wires sang the story across the country.[60] On June 19, a group of about two hundred armed men from Caddo Parish made their way across the Red River Bridge at Shreveport and rode to Benton. They surrounded the jail about midnight and, with a simple ruse that implied collusion, obtained the keys to the jail and took Smith and McLand north of Benton on the Arkansas Road. They hanged the men side by side.[61] The mob leaders proclaimed that the acts were necessary to preserve the lives of white men in the area.[62] Prince Edwards was never found, although several men were brought in over the years that were identified as the culprit. The crime set the stage for quick-response lynchings for violent crimes.

Beginning with Governor Heard and continuing with his successor, Shreveport native Newton Crain Blanchard, attempts were made to curb lynching. A victory for due process was found in the legal trial and execution of Charles Coleman on March 1, 1906, but lynchings continued.[63] Three years after Coleman's execution on November 27, 1909, a seven-year-old white girl, Jennie McMillan, was assaulted in a vacant house in Shreveport.[64] The little girl and her sister identified Simmie Rochelle as her attacker, and a "howling mob" of five hundred people took him away from Shreveport police officers to the twin Portland Street railroad bridges.[65] As officers tried to retrieve the suspect, they were brushed aside. Rochelle was found dangling from one of the railroad trestles. The *Shreveport Times* ran an extensive story on the incident, and the tone of the coverage, perhaps for the first time, was anti-lynching.[66]

The Caddo Parish Grand Jury was convened in mid-December to investigate the lynching. The district attorney, Thomas Fletcher Bell Jr., wanted murder convictions. There was no police report because the witnesses would not talk. One comment before the grand jury was that perhaps

Lynching of Jessie Hammett on August 26, 1916, in Vivian, Louisiana. *Courtesy of the Louisiana Oil and Gas Museum.*

Rochelle had really committed suicide by entangling his head in a piece of rope and jumping off the bridge. Another report implicated two men, both of whom had died in the intervening month.[67] Most people wanted the matter to end by default. The *New Orleans Item* agreed with the *Shreveport Times* in condemning the act.

The lynching of Simmie Rochelle occurred in broad daylight, and the men wore no masks or disguise of any sort. These facts, coupled with the further fact that a dozen policemen and deputy sheriffs fought the mob for half an hour in a vain effort to save the Negro's neck, may make it possible for at least the ringleaders of the mob to be identified.[68] Ultimately, the grand jury returned no indictments for the lynching. After seating two hundred witnesses, not one could provide the name or description of a single member of the lynch mob.[69] Due process remained an elusive concept.

Simmie Rochelle's lynching was not the last in northwestern Louisiana. Of the twenty-three additional events that occurred, one incident raised emotions to a higher level than the others. In late August 1916, a black man named Jessie Hammett was lynched in Vivian, Louisiana, in northern

Lynching: The Hard Hand of Swift Justice

The Portland Avenue Bridge in Shreveport from which Simmie Rochelle was lynched on November 28, 1909. *From* Louisiana: Its Street and Interurban Railways, *77.*

Caddo Parish. A crowd of more than one thousand people witnessed the lynching, and unlike most such events, it was photographed.

Hammett had worked for a wealthy family in town and had helped take care of their paraplegic daughter. Apparently, the two developed a relationship that was unknown to the family. On August 26, someone caught the couple either having sex or about to do so and spread the alarm that Hammett was raping the crippled teenager. He was arrested and taken to jail, where a mass mob grabbed Hammett and took him downtown to the corner of Pine Street and Louisiana Avenue. While Hammett was in jail, the girl's parents apparently talked to her and discovered that the sex was consensual. They went downtown and tried to talk the mob out of hanging Hammett. They were unsuccessful, and Hammett was hanged from a telegraph pole and left dangling as a lesson.[70] Although the common perception in the region was almost completely against miscegenation, this lynching seems to have tipped the balance in favor of due process. There would be no more mass lynchings in northwestern Louisiana.

Of the eight later lynchings, five were private, two were not identified by type and one was by a posse. Only one occurred in Caddo Parish. Three were for murder or attempted murder, two were for rape or attempted rape and three were for various forms of miscegenation. The last lynching in Caddo Parish occurred in 1923. This misguided act ended the rule of Judge Lynch in the parish. On January 8, 1923, a thirty-five-year-old man named Leslie Leggett was kidnapped from his rented room on Christian Street in Shreveport by a group of five masked men.[71] He was taken to the edge of town and "riddled with bullets."[72] The chief of police stated that Leggett had been arrested several times previously for associating with white women and had been booked as a black man.[73] Charles Papa, Leggett's employer, told the *Shreveport Times* that Leggett was a Spaniard.[74] This seemed to be the final act to turn the public away from lynching in Caddo Parish. Two years later, a lynching occurred in Bossier Parish from an unknown cause. On August 4, 1926, a black man was lynched by a posse for making improper advances to a white girl in DeSoto Parish.[75] The final lynching in the state of Louisiana occurred twenty years later, on August 8, 1946, when John Jones, a black man, was privately lynched for intent to rape in Webster Parish.[76] This put an end to a sordid dual system of informal versus legal executions in Louisiana.

3
The Ku Klux Klan in Northwest Louisiana

W. Chris Hale, PhD

Nothing in the world is more dangerous than sincere ignorance and conscientious stupidity.
—*Martin Luther King Jr.*

Ghosts of the Confederate Dead

Arising from the economic and social disorganization in the wake of the Civil War, six veterans of the Confederate army organized a small social club or fraternity. Their meeting took place in the summer of 1866, in the law office of Judge Thomas M. Jones of Pulaski, Tennessee. Apparently bored with small-town country life and longing for the thrills and heroics of war, Captain John C. Lester, Major James R. Crowe, John B. Kennedy, Calvin E. Jones, Richard R. Reed and Frank O. McCord organized the now infamous Ku Klux Klan.[77] Initially organized for amusement purposes only, the six former soldiers essentially engaged in horseplay, wearing disguises and riding their horses around town after dark. Finding that their actions frightened former and often superstitious slaves in the area, the members of the Pulaski Klan, thought to be ghosts of dead Confederate soldiers, heightened their activities in an attempt to restore the former plantation system. The idea of frightening former slaves back to work attracted numerous new members, resulting in the spread and rapid expansion of the Ku Klux Klan.[78] With dens[79] organizing across Tennessee and neighboring

General Nathan Bedford Forrest, Confederate general from Tennessee and first grand wizard of the Ku Klux Klan. *Library of Congress, Prints and Photographs Division.*

states, the founding Pulaski members sought to maintain some degree of central authority. Thus, in April 1867, a meeting took place in Nashville, Tennessee, to codify rules and organizational structure. At this time, former Confederate general Nathan Bedford Forrest was elected as the first grand wizard, or supreme ruler, of the Klan.[80]

Radical Reconstruction and the 1868 Presidential Election

Relatively nonviolent in nature, the Ku Klux Klan, under the leadership of Forrest, grew and transformed considerably following the passage of the Reconstruction Acts of March to July 1867. Seeking, among other objectives, to extend the rights of southern blacks, the South was essentially divided into five military districts, each controlled by a commanding general. Fearing and rejecting the authority of the hated radical Republican government, white and largely Democratic political and paramilitary organizations, including the Ku Klux Klan, rose up in violent opposition.[81] In fact, harassment, intimidation and murder became more commonplace, as northern teachers, judges, politicians, carpetbaggers and freedmen were targeted indiscriminately. Louisiana was no exception, as conservative whites organized into a number of secret paramilitary organizations, including, but not limited to, the Knights of the White Camellia, the Swamp Fox Rangers, the Innocents, the Seymour Knights, the Hancock Guards, the White League and the Ku Klux Klan.[82] Given the large number of groups operating in Louisiana, Allen Trelease argues that "it remained impossible to distinguish fully between the various organizations."[83] Likewise, Trelease concludes that "the situation was further confused by the common tendency to use the term Ku Klux generically to cover all of them."[84] Regardless of their chosen name, white group violence in Louisiana reached epic proportions in the months leading up to the 1868 presidential election.

    Hoping to elect Democrat Horatio Seymour over Republican candidate Ulysses S. Grant, Louisiana white paramilitary organizations, led by the Knights of the White Camellia (KWC), initiated a campaign of terror against freedmen never before witnessed in Louisiana. In obtaining a victory for Seymour at any cost, Louisiana conservatives felt, as many southerners, that a Democratic president would end Radical Reconstruction in the South.[85] Furthermore, the only way to obtain a Seymour victory in Louisiana was to ensure that everyone, including blacks, voted Democrat. Numerous techniques were utilized to encourage the black vote, ranging from economic intimidation to murder. For example, white landowners would oftentimes refuse employment of black sharecroppers who planned to vote Republican. If economic intimidation failed, hanging, drowning and shooting of blacks and radical whites were not uncommon. Given that blacks outnumbered whites almost three to one in northwest Louisiana,[86] controlling the black majority and securing the Democratic vote took on increasing importance for these groups.[87]

    Historically, violence was nothing new to residents of northwestern Louisiana. Shreveport, the largest town on the Red River, was a favored watering hole of Texas and Arkansas desperadoes and roughriders where disputes were often settled through violent confrontation. Shreveport was minimally affected by the Civil War and briefly served as the capital of

Confederate Louisiana. Area whites never really felt defeated and very much despised the Reconstruction policies of the federal government.[88] Thus, violence and intimidation of the majority black population was not only accepted but also justified. Realizing this fact, the KWC, Ku Klux Klan and other white paramilitary organizations easily spread and recruited members throughout northwest Louisiana. Indeed, in 1868, nearly every white adult male living in northwest Louisiana was a member of one of these groups.[89] Not only was white-on-black violence becoming an increasingly frequent occurrence, but also the attacks were often brutal in nature.

For example, in Claiborne Parish, approximately sixty miles northeast of Shreveport, a freedman representing the parish in the constitutional convention was assassinated in his yard on May 6, 1868.[90] Three weeks later, in neighboring Bienville Parish, a black Republican named Moses Lawhorn was dragged from his home and beheaded.[91] On October 1, 1868, nine black persons were thrown into the Red River. Told to swim for their lives, each was shot as he surfaced. Later that evening, thirty freedmen were lined along the banks of the Red River, tied together and shot in the back. On October 12, 1868, seven black persons burned alive after being chained in a building that was later set ablaze.[92] That same day, Solomon Thomas, a Shreveport freedman, witnessed the kidnapping and murder of four black men and a boy. Vicious in nature, the white gang cut holes into the hands of the victims, tied them together by running a rope through their hands, dragged them to the banks of the Red River and shot and drowned them.[93] Townspeople reported that it was not uncommon to see dead black persons floating down the river past Shreveport. In fact, in the month of October alone, witnesses saw twenty-five to thirty bodies in the Red River.[94] Also in Shreveport, in a brutal and sadistic attempt to teach Lucy Smith a lesson, a group of white men cut off one of her breasts. With their blood lust not satisfied, they proceeded to disembowel her and then remove her head. Finally, they threw her mutilated body into a nearby tree.[95] On election day, black men were forced at gunpoint to vote the Democratic ticket or risk death. Only one vote was cast for the Republican ticket of Grant and Colfax in Caddo Parish, and the voter, James Watson, was shot dead. In total, forty-two persons were murdered in Caddo Parish during the month of October alone.[96] Clearly, the number and nature of the deaths in Caddo, Claiborne and Bienville were appalling, but they pale in comparison to the weeklong slaughter of more than one hundred black persons in Bossier Parish in late September/early October 1868.

The Ku Klux Klan in Northwest Louisiana

On September 29, 1868, an intoxicated white Arkansas trader rode into Shady Grove Plantation and inquired as to whether there were any Republicans residing there. After an aging freedman was pointed out, the trader drew his gun, pointed it at the old man and fired off two rounds. Missing each time, the trader was captured by a black posse, who intended to turn him over to the proper authorities. Later that evening, a number of Bossier Parish citizens successfully freed the trader. The next day, the trader returned to Shady Grove with seventy-five to one hundred Arkansas men, all armed with revolvers, shotguns and rifles. Firing indiscriminately, they murdered eighteen men and three women. The women were wives of the men who were slaughtered in cold blood as they pleaded for their husbands' lives. Later that day, the armed band of white men began attacking the homes of black preachers. Made to swear that they would never preach again, each man was beaten so badly that he had to be carried home. Fearing a black uprising, white residents of Shreveport, as well as Bossier Parish planters, began arming themselves and set out to kill every black person with a gun. More a massacre than a fair fight, the armed bands of white men traveled from plantation to plantation, shooting men and women. Many were shot down as they picked cotton in the fields.[97] Although an exact number is difficult to ascertain, it has been estimated that more than one hundred freedmen lost their lives within a week or so of the Shady Gove incident. Finally, and similar to Caddo Parish, only one vote was cast for the Republican ticket of Grant and Colfax.

In summary, the Ku Klux movement's campaign of terror was largely successful and carried the state for the Democratic ticket of Seymour and Blair during the 1868 presidential election. Out of a total of 7,640 registered Republican voters in Bossier, Caddo, De Soto, Bienville and Sabine Parishes, only five votes were cast for Grant and Colfax.[98] Nevertheless, despite victories in Louisiana and six other states, Seymour and Blair lost to Grant and Colfax. Shortly thereafter, white-on-black violence fell sharply in northwestern Louisiana, only returning briefly in 1874.

THE WHITE LEAGUE MOVEMENT AND REDEMPTION

Convinced that Radical Republicans, consisting primarily of northern whites and southern blacks, were corrupt and incapable of governing Louisiana, frustrated Democratic whites organized the White League. Most

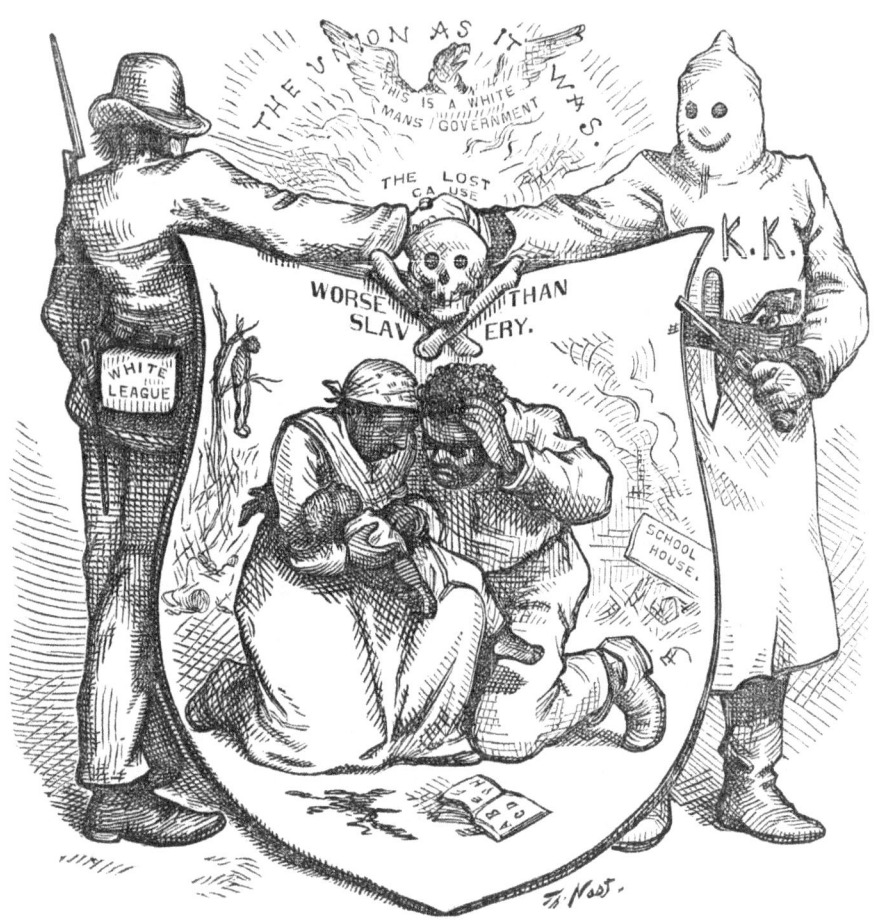

An 1874 political cartoon by Thomas Nast for *Harper's Weekly* depicting a man from the White League shaking hands with a Ku Klux Klan member. *Library of Congress, Prints and Photographs Division.*

likely born in Alexandria, Louisiana, after the publication of a manifesto in the *Alexandria Caucasian*, the White League soon spread to nearly every parish in the state.[99] Published on March 28, 1874, the manifesto proclaimed, "There will be no security, no peace, and no prosperity for Louisiana until… the superiority of the Caucasian over the African in all affairs pertaining to government, is acknowledged and established."[100] Less than a month later, the first White League meeting was held in Opelousas. The second meeting took place in Mansfield, about forty miles south of Shreveport.[101] Encouraged by articles in the *Shreveport Times*, the White League hunted, terrorized and lynched blacks throughout the summer of 1874.[102] One freedman, alleged to have killed a white man, was covered with turpentine, shot and set on fire. Black clergymen were murdered, and black churches were regularly burned to the ground.[103] Caddo officials reported at least thirty murders in July and August alone.[104] Not immune to the violence, white Republican officeholders were terrorized and forced to resign their positions. In Coushatta, six whites, including Homer Twitchell, brother of Senator Marshall Twitchell, were brutally murdered on August 30, 1874.[105] Known as the Coushatta Massacre, five Republican officeholders and M.C. Willis were being escorted from the state when a mob of White League members came upon them. The mob, led by "Captain Jack" Dick Coleman, shot and then mutilated the bodies of all six men.[106] Violent attacks such as these continued for the remainder of the year, eventually forcing Governor Kellogg to request the presence of U.S. troops during the election of 1874.[107] Violence continued for nearly three years as Louisiana White League members finally "redeemed" Louisiana with a Democratic win in 1877.[108] Shortly thereafter, in 1879–80, approximately five thousand freedmen, many from Caddo, migrated to Kansas.[109]

Regardless of their chosen name, the Ku Klux Klan, the Knights of the White Camellia, the White League and other white paramilitary organizations carried out campaign violence and terror against blacks and radical whites for more than a decade in northwest Louisiana. With overlapping membership and similar ceremonies and rituals, these groups threatened, assaulted and murdered countless persons to restore white supremacy and a conservative Democratic government. Successfully accomplishing their goals, the organizations eventually disbanded. Relatively quiet for almost forty years, the Ku Klux movement returned with a vengeance in the 1920s.

THE ROARING TWENTIES

Recovering in an Atlanta hospital bed after being hit by a car, William Joseph Simmons outlined his plans for a new fraternal order to be called the Invisible Empire, Knights of the Ku Klux Klan, Inc. He was inspired by the 1915 release of the silent film *The Birth of a Nation*. The film, directed by D.W. Griffith, depicted blacks as violent rapists and the Reconstruction-era Klan as heroic saviors of the South. Advertising through newspapers and word of mouth, Simmons gradually recruited around ninety people. Each new member was required to pay a $10.00 initiation fee and buy a robe costing $60.50. By 1917, the Invisible Empire had spread to only neighboring Alabama and had a membership of approximately 5,000. Unhappy with the slow growth of the order, Simmons turned to a publicity company to help him boost recruitment efforts. Understanding the attraction of secrecy, ceremony and costumes, the plan was to divide the entire county into "domains," or groups of states, that were headed by a "grand goblin." Each state would be referred to as a "realm" and was headed by a "grand dragon." All realms were further divided into districts, or "provinces," headed by a "great titan." All local groups, or chapters, met in a "klavern" and used a ritual book known as the "Kloran" to open and close meetings. Elected by chapter members, the head of a chapter, known as the "exalted Cyclops," served a one-year term. "Kleagles," or field recruitment officers, solicited new members by exploiting regional prejudices and earned a commission of $4.00 out of each new "klectoken," or $10.00 initiation fee. The strategy worked as Klan membership spread and grew by nearly 100,000 members in 1921.[110]

A Ku Klux Klan initiation ceremony on Black Lake near Coushatta, Louisiana. *Archives and Special Collections, Noel Memorial Library, Louisiana State University in Shreveport.*

The Ku Klux Klan in Northwest Louisiana

Spreading rapidly throughout the South, the Ku Klux Klan reentered Louisiana and began organizing a chapter in New Orleans in November 1920.[111] The chapter's name was Old Hickory Klan Number One and consisted of lawyers, politicians and doctors. Approximately one week later, Shreveport Klan Number Two was established. Given its rural nature and the large number of protestant whites, Shreveport became the state headquarters of the Louisiana Klan. In fact, a Shreveport lumberman by the name of Carey P. Duncan was appointed Grand Dragon.[112] Also in Shreveport, the Louisiana Klan made its first public appearance as it paraded through the city on April 9, 1921.[113] Shortly thereafter, the Klan spread from Shreveport into the smaller cities and towns of northern Louisiana. The Klan also spread, although more cautiously, into predominantly Catholic southern Louisiana.

As the Klan spread throughout the state, most members became increasingly unconcerned with the national aims of the Ku Klux Klan. In general, the Louisiana Klan, at this time, was not concerned with

A Ku Klux Klan meeting on Black Lake near Coushatta, Louisiana. *Archives and Special Collections, Noel Memorial Library, Louisiana State University in Shreveport.*

immigration, the Jewish problem or white supremacy and thought of itself as more of a moralistic law enforcement agency.[114] The Klan took it upon itself to clean up society and punish bootleggers, moonshiners, vagrants, gamblers and prostitutes, black or white. For example, after Shreveport police released wife beater Jack Morgan on May 25, 1921, Klansmen hooded Morgan and took him to Mooringsport Road. They then stripped him naked and covered him with tar and feathers.[115] Religion was also important to Louisiana Klansmen, as some of the most prominent leaders were ordained Protestant ministers. Dr. E.L. Thompson, the exalted Cyclops of Shreveport Klan Number Two, was the pastor of the Central Christian Church in Shreveport.[116] Likewise, because of the Protestant nature of the Klan, Catholicism was a chief concern. Klansmen, at least in northern Louisiana, carried and distributed "Do You Know" cards. These cards listed fifteen assertions essentially claiming that the pope was a political autocrat, hell-bent on dominating the government of the United States.[117]

Not only did religion act as a strong bond between members, but also the fraternal nature of the order was important to Louisiana Klansmen. Rituals, secret ceremonies and the ability to network were strong selling points of the Klan. Social events were also important as Klan parades were often spectacular in nature. For example, in September 1923, Shreveport hosted the big Konklave.[118] At this event, Klansmen from all over Louisiana and surrounding states took part in a large rally followed by fireworks. The crowd then witnessed a parade of three thousand Shreveport Klansmen followed by the burning of a thirty-foot wooden cross. As the cross burned, the capacity crowd sang both religious and patriotic songs.[119] Events such as these were common throughout 1923 and 1924, as the Invisible Empire was at its strongest both politically and in sheer numbers. Louisiana alone boasted twenty-five to thirty thousand members.[120]

After climaxing in 1924, the Invisible Empire as a whole began to crumble. Whether it was due to violent acts resulting in poor public image or dissension among members, the 1920s Klan eventually broke into several competing independent realms. Klan membership in Louisiana alone dropped below three thousand members. This was most likely due to the passage of anti-Klan legislation led by Governor Fuqua in May 1924.[121] The Klan never really recovered, as membership continued to plummet throughout the 1940s, 1950s and 1960s. Although the civil rights movement sparked minor Klan activity in Louisiana, law enforcement was quick to respond.[122] With only a

The Ku Klux Klan in Northwest Louisiana

A Ku Klux Klan rally at Oil City in the 1970s. *Courtesy of the Louisiana Oil and Gas Museum.*

few thousand members nationally, the once-powerful Klan was driven into the cornfields and pastures of America. However, as the 1970s approached, a handsome, young, intelligent and motivated Louisianan fought to improve the image of the Klan.

OUT OF THE COW PASTURES: THE KLAN GOES MAINSTREAM

David Duke, imperial wizard and instigator of the 1974 revival of the Ku Klux Klan, once stated that "we've got to get out of the cow pasture and into the hotel meeting rooms." Duke, born on July 1, 1950, in Tulsa, Oklahoma, moved with his family to New Orleans in the 1960s. After high school, he attended Louisiana State University (LSU), where he privately studied white supremacy and anti-Semitism. While a student, he was also a member of the Independent Knights of the Ku Klux Klan. He eventually

Police remove a burned Ku Klux Klan cross from the lawn of U.S. representative Overton Brooks's (D-La.) home in Shreveport, Louisiana. *Archives and Special Collections, Noel Memorial Library, Louisiana State University in Shreveport.*

graduated from LSU with a degree in history and became leader of his Klan chapter. Understanding the value of media, Duke participated in television, radio and magazine interviews. He recruited on college campuses and even allowed women and Catholics to become members. Duke preferred to be called national director as opposed to imperial wizard. He often refused to wear the traditional white robe and stressed nonviolent opposition. Duke felt that government participation was the only way to improve conditions, arguing that the affirmative action and forced busing programs of the 1960s unfairly victimized whites. Under his leadership, Klan membership rose and boasted a national membership of 3,500 people.[123] Nevertheless, despite Duke's attempt to revive the organization to its former 1920s glory, scandals, violence and differences in ideology continued to decimate the Klan.

The Ku Klux Klan in Northwest Louisiana

Today's Ku Klux Klan

Currently, there are approximately thirteen white hate organizations operating in Louisiana. This includes two neo-Nazi groups, two Christian identity groups, one neo-Confederate group, one racist skinhead group, three white nationalist groups and four Ku Klux Klan groups. Most of the Klan groups can be found in the northern and central part of the state and include the Brotherhood of Klans Knights of the Ku Klux Klan, Dixie Rangers Knights of the Ku Klux Klan, United Northern and Southern Knights of the Ku Klux Klan and the United White Knights of the Ku Klux Klan. The United White Knights of the Ku Klux Klan have a strong presence in northwest Louisiana, with chapters in Shreveport, Homer, Monroe and Sarepta. Shreveport is also home to two white nationalist groups, the United Patriots and Associates and the Council of Conservative Citizens.[124] Pushing a victimization agenda, principal concerns include a fear that whites are becoming a numerical minority and a fear that whites are losing social authority and power. More specifically, Klan rhetoric focuses on perceived legal sanctions against whites (e.g., affirmative action), perceived attacks on Christian values (e.g., homosexuals) and immigration (e.g., job loss). In addition, today's Klan uses the Internet to spread messages of hate and violence, gather and share information, raise funds, recruit new members, network and garner publicity.

Conclusion

In closing, it is worth discussing a 2009 report prepared by the Extremism and Radicalization Branch, Homeland Environment Threat Analysis Division. This report suggests the right-wing-extremist Internet chatter indicates that "the economic downturn and the election of the first African American president present unique drivers for rightwing radicalization and recruitment."[125] The report further argues that the three officers killed in Pittsburgh, Pennsylvania, on April 4, 2009, by a racist gunman and the planned but disrupted attack on then senator Barack Obama in the run-up to the 2008 presidential election point to an escalation in right-wing extremist violence. Clearly, the nearly 150-year racist and often violent history of the Ku Klux Klan points to the need to remain vigilant in understanding the ideologies and actions of these groups.

4
Blind Tigers and Bootlegging in Caddo Parish During Prohibition

W. Chris Hale, PhD

When I sell liquor, it's called bootlegging; when my patrons serve it on Lake Shore Drive, it's called hospitality.
—Al Capone

THE NOBLE EXPERIMENT

A few minutes before midnight on January 16, 1920, Americans in bars and saloons across the country finished their beers and sipped the remaining drops of whiskey from their glasses. As the clock struck midnight, policemen and Prohibition-enforcement officers entered drinking establishments and hotels and began confiscating the now illegal alcohol. In many large cities, bar owners and saloonkeepers wishing to remain open were intimidated and threatened and told to close or have their doors padlocked shut for a year's time.[126] Liquor stores had nothing left to confiscate, as customers had filled cars, trucks, wagons and baby buggies with large quantities of alcohol to be stored for private use.[127] Thirteen breweries in St. Louis were forced to close, and the great distilleries of Peoria, Illinois, were to be converted to food-processing plants.[128] As thirsty city dwellers made their way home, unable or unwilling to comprehend present events, rural Americans celebrated. In fact, thousands of God-fearing people attended prayer meetings in Protestant churches across already dry territories and rejoiced in victory over the reviled "demon rum."[129] Ready or not, the "Noble Experiment" had begun.

Fully ratified by January 16, 1919, and becoming effective on January 17, 1920, the Eighteenth Amendment banned the manufacture, sale and transportation of intoxicating liquors.[130] Enforced through the Volstead Act, intoxicating liquors were defined as any beverage containing more than one-half of 1 percent of alcohol. The Volstead Act also established procedures and agencies of enforcement, assigning responsibility to the Internal Revenue Bureau in the Department of the Treasury.[131] Shortly thereafter, a rising criminal class, corruption, scandals and changing social and cultural patterns resulted in a wealth of problems for those wishing to enforce the newly enacted national Prohibition laws. Already dealing with prohibition for more than eleven years, Caddo Parish and the city of Shreveport were no exception.

Shreveport Goes Dry

On January 14, 1908, in what was described as the "Most Exciting Election in the History of the Parish,"[132] Caddo parishioners, by a majority of only sixty-six, voted in favor of prohibition. Although the majority of voters within the city limits of Shreveport were anti-prohibition, the rural prohibitionists, larger in number, took the election. According to the newspaper reporter, nearly five thousand men, women and children assembled and watched the bulletins. The reporter further added that cheering, for both sides, could be heard for almost ten blocks.[133] After the election, the prohibitionists waved banners and paraded through the city. The anti-prohibitionists were led by former mayor Andrew Querbes, Captain Peter Youree, Dr. Ashton Blanchard (son of then governor Newton C. Blanchard) and attorney John D. Wilkinson.[134] They argued that prohibition would result in $180,000 in lost city revenues, which would have otherwise been generated from liquor licensing. Furthermore, these losses would have a negative impact on police operations and other city departments, eventually resulting in property loss and death-like conditions.[135] They predicted that the city would be filled with criminals and blind tigers,[136] as the flourishing legal liquor trade would move to Texarkana, Monroe, Alexandria and Marshall.

The prohibitionists, on the other hand, were led by Reverends Claude L. Jones and Jasper K. Smith, Councilman L.C. Allen and Colonel John B. Young. They argued that saloons distracted men from God and were responsible for societal ills such as poverty and crime.[137] The prohibitionists led prayer meetings and gave more than three hundred speeches in the six weeks preceding the vote.[138] Victorious, the era of prohibition in Caddo Parish would begin on January 1, 1909.[139] Also going into effect in 1909 was the Gay-Shattuck Law. The Gay-Shattuck had three primary objectives. Along with segregating blacks and whites in drinking establishments, the law forbade gambling in saloons and prohibited liquor sales within three hundred feet of schools and churches.[140]

Caddo Prohibition League. *Precinct No. 3 Prohibition Club Attendance Log Book.* Archives and Special Collections, Noel Memorial Library, Louisiana State University in Shreveport.

A Model Prohibition City

Shortly thereafter, on October 2, 1909, Shreveport district attorney J.M. Foster facilitated a dragnet that resulted in the arrest of forty alleged sellers of illegal alcohol. As deputy sheriffs and policemen carried out their duties, many of the illegal sellers were seen running from their businesses in attempts to evade capture. The businesses included the Caddo and Phoenix Hotel bars, the Manhattan, the Hub, Big Casino, Peerless and Ninety-Nine. Each violator was given a bond of $350. Those unable to pay went directly to jail.[141] According to the reporter covering the incident, "The scene in the Sheriff's office…was one that has never been paralleled here."[142] On June 16, 1910, Shreveport physician Dr. T.F. Long became the first physician charged with violating prohibition law. Apparently, Long wrote a prescription for whiskey, knowing it was not needed for medicinal purposes.[143] On January 31, 1911, Shreveport police destroyed a wagonload of whiskey that was seized from blind tiger raids.[144] A few months later, a Shreveport detective opened up a blind tiger in an attempt to infiltrate and "get next" to prohibition law violators. As a result, fourteen persons were arrested and sentenced to ninety days on a chain gang. In addition, all were fined $850. Among the prohibition violators, five were former members of the police department, including former police chief J.B. McCormick.[145] Similar arrests and sentencing of an additional eight blind tiger operators occurred in the summer of 1912.[146]

Despite aggressive attempts to bring violators to justice, angry Caddo citizens held a massive city hall meeting on February 9, 1913. Reacting to a report prepared by the Caddo Grand Jury, meeting participants demanded more vigorous law enforcement. According to the report, vice conditions in Shreveport were deplorable as gambling and prohibition laws were being openly and flagrantly violated. Resolutions were adopted demanding that top law enforcement officials be held more accountable for non-enforcement. Meeting participants also suggested that officers not doing their duty should be forced to resign. Courts were asked to hand out maximum punishments and be more willing to convict on circumstantial evidence. In addition, courts were urged to have more timely trials, as witnesses often disappeared. The meeting adjourned shortly after adopting a resolution that would petition the Louisiana delegation in Congress to vote in favor of the Webb-Kenyon Bill.[147] The law, passed that same year, effectively banned the shipment of intoxicating liquors into dry territories.[148]

Determined now more than ever to punish prohibition law violators, the City of Shreveport enacted the Fullilove "blind tiger" ordinance. This ordinance essentially declared a place where liquor was found to be a nuisance[149] and thus subject to search and seizure in an effort to abate that nuisance. In one of their first attempts to enforce the new ordinance, city commissioner S.C. Fullilove and police chief F.H. Lucar were informed that a large quantity of liquor was hidden on the premises of the old Joe

Blind Tigers and Bootlegging in Caddo Parish During Prohibition

Maroun Saloon. Given this information, they secured a search warrant. Upon arrival, they broke open a vault and discovered one thousand gallons of whiskey and gin. An arrest warrant was secured, and Maroun was arrested. That same day, four other men were arrested after sworn affidavits resulted in search warrants and subsequent raids of their Douglas Island establishments.[150] Determined to fight the constitutionality of the new ordinance, alleged blind tiger operators began filing injunction suits to prevent the police department from searching their premises. They argued that search warrants granted under the Fullilove ordinance were given on insufficient evidence. Nonetheless, on April 2, 1913, district judge T.F. Bell upheld the constitutionality of the new law, arguing that the city council "had the authority to adopt such regulations as were necessary in making the prohibition law effective."[151] Unfortunately, victory would be short-lived, as Shreveport cops would soon be accused of graft.

On July 3, 1913, during the trial of near beer dealer D.M. Ward, Ward stated that he paid "hush money" to two well-known Shreveport officers. The officers accused of taking bribes included Detective D.D. Bazar and Sergeant Will Daniels. Ward was a proprietor of a black near beer and poolroom establishment and allegedly paid ten dollars weekly

Bottles and a barrel of confiscated whiskey. *Library of Congress, Prints and Photographs Division.*

in "hush coin" in return for lax enforcement of Caddo prohibition laws. Nevertheless, Bazar and Daniels raided the establishment and arrested several of the patrons. Ward, wanting the charges dropped, informed Bazar that "his attitude would cost him his job." Ward then took his books and informed Commissioner Fullilove about the alleged bribe payments. Interestingly, the bribe payments were investigated and promptly ignored, and Ward was acquitted of the prohibition law violations. Not satisfied with the matter being dropped, Judge Land wanted an explanation as to why Ward was not charged after admitting to bribing officers. Apparently, no explanation was given.[152]

For the next few years, Caddo continued to aggressively enforce its prohibition laws. For example, on June 29, 1915, police raided several blind tiger establishments operating throughout the city. In total, twenty-seven persons, most of whom were of Assyrian or Italian descent, were arrested for liquor law violations.[153] Nine months later, sheriff deputies raided an Oil City establishment, resulting in the largest liquor seizure in Caddo prohibition history.[154] In total, the deputies seized twelve barrels of whiskey, nine casks of beer and fourteen three-gallon demijohns of whiskey. With the seized liquor valued at approximately $1,200, the four men were arrested and charged with operating a blind tiger.[155] Relentlessly pursued, blind tiger operators became increasingly inventive in hiding their crimes.

For example, on December 19, 1915, detectives "uncovered the most unusual alleged bootlegging establishment that has come to the attention of officials since this section of the state embraced prohibition."[156] The establishment, located on Linwood Avenue, was an orphan asylum run by Mrs. Van Cleave. Apparently, the asylum was a front for a bootlegging operation and contained several casks of beer and other liquors. Neighbors reported seeing numerous cars going in and out of the facility but never saw children. Interestingly, no arrests were made, as this establishment was located in "an aristocratic section of the city."[157] In another raid, police found that Shreveport bootleggers were hiding whiskey in dirty laundry tubs. According to the newspaper report, whiskey was placed in tightly corked bottles and lowered into the dirty tub water. In order to complete the illusion, the violators would then throw a few items of dirty clothes on top of the bottles.[158] Finally, in one of the most imaginative methods to date, local Department of Justice operatives arrested and charged four men with shipping intoxicating liquors into dry territories.[159] Basically, the violators

Blind Tigers and Bootlegging in Caddo Parish During Prohibition

were shipping alcohol from New Orleans, via Monroe, to Waco, Texas, in a coffin. The men, two undertakers and two physicians, loaded the coffin with liquor and attached a certificate stating that the pine box contained "the dead body of Jules Crawford." The coffin, shipped from New Orleans, was discovered in Fort Worth. "The coffin box looked innocent enough, but the snug appearance of the bereaved relative is said to have aroused the suspicion of officers."[160] The four men were charged with issuing false certificates, while the "bereaved relative" escaped. Although these bootleggers were captured, rumrunning out of New Orleans into nearby dry parishes and counties thrived in the early 1900s.[161] Therefore, not only was Caddo law enforcement dealing with its own parishioners, but it was dealing with fairly cunning outsiders as well. This resulted in numerous arrests and increased expenditures.

For example, Caddo recorded nearly 3,400 arrests during a five-year period ranging from 1909 to 1913.[162] Given that only 2,182 arrests occurred in the five years prior (1904–8), the number of arrests increased by more than 1,000 persons since prohibition began. There were 1,234 arrests in

Officials pouring confiscated whiskey into a sewer. *Library of Congress, Prints and Photographs Division.*

1913 alone. Likewise, criminal justice expenditures increased from $17,498 in 1905 to a predicted $65,000 by year's end in 1915.[163] Courts were quickly becoming overburdened with blind tiger and bootlegging cases, and a new $25,000 to $30,000 jail "had become an imperative necessity, mainly to care for the many bootleggers."[164] Anti-prohibitionists claimed that aggressive prohibition policies in Caddo were essentially turning formerly law-abiding and respectable citizens into criminals, while progressives from all over the nation pointed to Shreveport as a "model prohibition city."[165]

THE PROGRESSIVE MOVEMENT

Building out of and from the temperance movement, progressivism flourished for nearly thirty years, from 1890 to 1920. Progressives, largely middle-class Americans, sought to cure social and economic ills through governmental policies. Believing that alcohol use led to poor physical and mental health and reduced worker efficiency, progressives yearned for prohibition. In his 1918 work entitled *Why Prohibition!*, Reverend Charles Stelzle argued that America would not advance until alcohol was banished from its shores.[166] As a leading progressive, Stelzle argued that drinking led to industrial inefficiency and therefore was responsible for poor worker wages. In addition, drinking led to poor health and death, directly resulting in higher insurance rates for all Americans. He further argued that police, courts, corrections, hospitals and insane asylums generated at least half of their business from alcohol-related problems. This resulted in increased taxes for all Americans, as funds had to be raised to support these institutions. Due to these facts, Stelzle concluded that the social and economic costs for all Americans outweighed any one individual right or the pleasure one might derive from drinking intoxicating beverages.[167]

Businessmen and manufacturers agreed with these arguments, believing that prohibition would reduce accidents and increase worker efficiency and effectiveness.[168] Utilizing these arguments, progressives credited prohibition as responsible for Shreveport's economic prosperity in the early 1900s.[169] Nevertheless, one anti-prohibitionist pointed out that "prohibition had nothing to do with making oil come out of the ground, nor did it have anything to do with chasing the boll weevil out of the country."[170]

World War I

Regardless of the power of the progressive movement, it would take an act of war to ignite national Prohibition. Approximately three years after the first shot was fired, America entered World War I on April 6, 1917. As our soldiers fought, a temporary spirit of wartime sacrifice entered America. Prohibitionists promptly pointed out that a large quantity of grain was needed to produce alcohol. Given that prohibition would ban alcohol, America would conserve its grain resources. Not to mention, beer was synonymous with hated Germany.[171] Utilizing these arguments, Congress passed the Lever Food and Fuel Control Act on August 10, 1917. This act essentially outlawed the production of grain alcohol for the remainder of the war.[172] About this same time, Congress began considering an amendment to the Constitution that would effectively ban, once and for all, the manufacture, sale and transportation of intoxicating liquors. The Senate approved the Eighteenth Amendment on August 1, 1917, by a vote of 65 to 20. Approximately one month later, the House approved the amendment by a vote of 282 to 128. The proposed Eighteenth Amendment then awaited ratification by legislatures in at least three-fourths of the states. While waiting for state legislators to affirm the new amendment, the War Prohibition Act of November 18, 1918, was passed. This act banned the manufacture and sale of any and all intoxicating beverages of more than 2.75 percent alcohol until demobilization.[173]

Louisiana Considers Prohibition

In the summer of 1918, Louisiana legislators met in a special session to reconsider the Eighteenth Amendment. Given that the Senate had been deadlocked twenty to twenty during an earlier session, legislators hoped that the tie would be broken one way or another. With nearly thirty Louisiana parishes, including Caddo, already dry, the prohibition question was already answered with a resounding yes. These thirty parishes contained 52.9 percent of the population and consisted of more than 80.0 percent of the state's territories.[174] Shreveport was the state headquarters for the Anti-Saloon League, which was victorious in bringing prohibition to Caddo in 1909.[175] Monroe in Ouachita Parish, the last "wet spot between Texas and the District of Columbia," was dry by 1917.[176] In direct opposition to the mostly Protestant northern parishes, southern parishes were Catholic and largely anti-prohibition in nature. Not to mention that America's wettest city, New Orleans, resided in southern Louisiana. The difference in opinion was so strong that Robert Ewing, publisher of both the *New Orleans States* and the *Shreveport Times*, remained neutral in the *Times* while criticizing prohibitionists in the *States*.[177]

Deadlocked at twenty to twenty, the tie was broken on August 6, 1918, when the Louisiana Senate passed the ratification measure by a vote of twenty-one to twenty. Two days later, Louisiana ratified the Eighteenth Amendment when the House voted sixty-nine to forty-one in its favor.[178] Upon hearing the news, Reverend A.W. Turner of Shreveport, leader of the Louisiana Anti-Saloon League, proclaimed, "We have won fairly and left no scars. We won without the help of the *Shreveport Times* and with the opposition of the *New Orleans States*."[179] Ratified by all states by January 16, 1919, national Prohibition became effective on January 17, 1920. As the most rapidly approved amendment in the history of the United States, the Eighteenth Amendment was ratified by forty-four state legislatures in only thirteen months.[180] While it remained business as usual in northern Louisiana, 99,991 gallons of whiskey and 1,332,380 gallons of alcohol sailed out of the port of New Orleans, headed toward South America.[181]

Repealing National Prohibition

On January 17, 1920, the focused shifted from Shreveport and other model prohibition cities to Chicago, New York and similar prohibition war zones. Enforcing prohibition laws frequently turned violent, and prohibition gangsters, such as Al Capone, Vito Genovese and Charles "Lucky" Luciano, often dominated newspaper headlines. Gang turf battles killed 500 people in Chicago and more than 1,000 in New York. In the 1920s alone, approximately 137 people were killed by federal prohibition agents.[182] Bribery, extortion and embezzlement were common, resulting in 1 out every 12 agents being dismissed by 1926. When enforcement was transferred from the Internal Revenue Bureau in the Department of Treasury to the Justice Department in 1930, three-fourths of the agents were unable to pass the civil service exam.[183] The criminal justice system

Blind Tigers and Bootlegging in Caddo Parish During Prohibition

Two men standing outdoors with a small still; one of them is holding up a bottle of liquor. *Library of Congress, Prints and Photographs Division.*

was rapidly overwhelmed, as prohibition cases flooded the courts. Jails and prisons were overcrowded to the point that they had to release convicted offenders. To make matters worse, the Ku Klux Klan thought it was the Klan's duty to clean up society and often carried out vigilante justice on bootleggers, moonshiners and gamblers.[184]

Those unable or unwilling to buy illegal liquor made their own. Homemade stills were common as pharmacies gladly provided all the necessary ingredients. In fact, ingredients such as yeast, juniper oil, iodine and caramel were readily available. In addition, anything and everything containing liquor flew off the store shelves, including embalming fluid, antifreeze and rubbing alcohol.[185] People would buy grape juice or concentrates and allow them to ferment. Thanks to distributor "warning" labels, purchasers knew that after the product sat out for sixty days, it would turn into wine.[186] Near beer, or beer containing the approved .5 percent alcohol, would be converted into "needle beer." Needle beer was near beer that had alcohol injected into the container after government inspection. Finally, and for "medicinal purposes" only, people could obtain alcohol by means of a prescription. These prescriptions were provided by the more than fifteen thousand doctors and fifty-seven thousand pharmacists who obtained liquor licenses in the first six months of Prohibition alone.[187] Without a doubt, crime, corruption and a general willingness to break the law pointed to America's true love affair with alcohol. As the 1920s came to end and the Great Depression began, Americans wanted change.

For many across the United States, the Noble Experiment was a failure. Therefore, the Senate approved the Twenty-first Amendment to repeal Prohibition on February 16, 1933, by a vote of 63 to 23. Approximately four days later, the House approved the new amendment by a vote of 289 to 121. The proposed Twenty-first Amendment then awaited ratification by legislatures in at least three-fourths of the states.[188] Of the nearly twenty-one million Americans polled between April and November 1933, 73 percent favored repeal.[189] Similar to national sentiment, Louisianans also sought to change the prohibition laws. A 1930 *Literary Digest* poll found that 77 percent of those polled were in favor of change. Two years later, that percentage rose five points to 82 percent favoring repeal.[190] In addition, Louisiana citizens voted to repeal the Hood Act in a 1932 referendum election. Passed in 1921, the act essentially enacted the terms of the federal Volstead Act into Louisiana state law. Fulfilling their wishes, the Louisiana legislature abolished the Hood Act on March 24, 1933, essentially repealing state prohibition laws.[191] Shortly thereafter, the federal Volstead Act was amended on April 7, 1933, making beer legal again. Approximately eight months later, Utah became the thirty-sixth state to ratify the new Twenty-first Amendment, effectively repealing the Eighteenth Amendment.[192]

5
The Red-Light District in Shreveport

Cheryl H. White, PhD

It shall not be lawful for any woman or girl who is known to be a lewd person to stand upon the sidewalk in front of the premises occupied by her.
—Shreveport Council, An Ordinance Relating to Lewd Women, *1871*

Prostitution has not only existed since the dawn of recorded history, but it also permeates the mythology and legend of every ancient society. The earliest historical record of prostitution may date to the biblical texts ascribed to Moses some eighteen centuries before the birth of Christ.[193] Such evidence in history and legend lends credibility to the often-repeated claim that prostitution is the oldest-known profession. The selling of sexual activity has been simultaneously embraced and condemned by societies in which the trade took hold, representing a practice that was usually profitable but carried social costs. Yet it has historically been a business enterprise that naturally follows wherever man settles in a community. Such was certainly the case in Shreveport, where a legal "red-light district" operated from 1903 to 1917, although prostitution existed in the city from the time the first settlers came in the early nineteenth century. When the era of the prostitution district drew to a close in 1917, national health authorities recognized Shreveport as having the largest such district among all cities of comparable size in the nation.[194]

Societies have not universally viewed prostitution as an illegal activity. Although practitioners of this ancient business have generally held a lesser place in society, the activity has not always been against the law. While many ancient, medieval and early modern societies had laws regulating adultery in the strictest sense, fornication does not have the same history of precedent in English common law, which shaped this country. However, "lewdness" is a term that is found in both English common law and in American law, as is the "keeping of a bawdy house." Interestingly, neither a legal definition of lewdness nor a bawdy house could be found anywhere in Louisiana law at the turn of the twentieth century.[195] However, a Shreveport city ordinance of December 1871 certainly addressed the issue in an attempt to keep prostitution out of the public sphere. In "An Ordinance Relating to and to Regulate Lewd Women," the council stated clearly that it "shall not be lawful for any woman or girl who is known to be a lewd person to stand upon the sidewalk in front of the premises occupied by her." The ordinance also stated that "no woman or girl who is notoriously known to be a lewd person shall be found to be strolling in any street, sidewalk, market house or alley, or drinking in any coffey [sic] house or saloon after 8:00 p.m. at night."[196]

An emphasis on appropriate times of day for prostitution activity dates from the earliest period of American history. Records from the colonial period reveal pervasive social concern about unseemly human activity in the hours after dark. In Massachusetts, "night walking" was a punishable offense.[197] However, the overall concern seems to have centered not on the sexual activity itself, but on the close relationship the activity had with vagrancy and related issues of public health. In fact, it was the concern for public health, not issues of morality, that first drove legislation against prostitution in the United States in the late nineteenth century. Rising cases of venereal diseases and the specter of a global war that required a healthy male population to take up arms probably contributed much to the first significant attempts to outlaw prostitution, but not before urban areas attempted instead to contain it, regulate it and profit from its practice.

Given the nature of prostitution's predictable history, it was no surprise that the industry flourished in a town such as Shreveport. It was a city that naturally attracted travelers, merchants and strangers passing through. Before the creation of a segregated red-light district, prostitution thrived on the riverfront of Shreveport in an area known as "the Batture" (or riverbank) located near the docks. Large brothels operated in the riverfront area from the earliest days of the city's growth in the 1830s. By the time the Shreveport City Council established a legal district for prostitution in an area of the city in Shreveport history. Known as simply "the Madam" and "the Queen of St. Paul's Bottoms," she operated quite profitably and powerfully even before the creation of the official red-light district. Although not much is known of her early years, McCune came to Shreveport during the Civil War, perhaps with Union troops up the Red River from New Orleans following the occupation of that city. Born in Ireland in 1840, her family may have been among the large numbers of Irish immigrants who sought refuge in America during the potato famines of the mid-nineteenth century. Biographers speculate that she may have resorted to prostitution as a means of survival.[203]

Historical records of Annie McCune's influence in Shreveport are somewhat scarce. A biographical framework within city history can be constructed from building deeds and other public records, but much of her personal life and story is unknown. Her first address within the city was listed on Common Street in downtown, and at least one brush with the law was recorded early on when, in the 1870s, she was arrested and fined for "streetwalking." Through legend and popularized myth surrounding her, there emerges an image of a kind but pragmatic businesswoman who cared for her women and her community. A persistent legend continues to posit that Annie McCune opened her house of ill repute as a hospital to victims of the city's yellow fever epidemic and that she herself nursed the ill and dying.[204] The 1900 United States Census lists her as the head of her household, with an occupation as "hotel keeper." Living with her at the time were two young female "boarders," with occupations listed as "seamstress" and "dressmaker."[205]

The historical setting and the intriguing personalities of the principals lends a distinct credibility to the commercial sex district of Shreveport. Once the city established the red-light district, McCune and two other madams, Nell Jester and Bea Haywood, began a profitable and well-maintained business of the world's oldest profession. By using the term "female boardinghouse," those operating within the red-light district maintained a level of propriety even within the illicit culture. This euphemism appears on historical maps and other documents of the early twentieth century and generally refers to a brothel, although it is unknown if record officials originated this term under pressure from local authorities or if the owners of the houses described their businesses in this manner.[206] It is an interesting commentary on the social norm under which such brothels operated, as the avoidance of the traditional language of prostitution indicates the level of legitimacy conferred to the establishments.

The Red-Light District in Shreveport

The segregation theory suggests that prostitution is a social evil that can nevertheless be contained and controlled, thereby protecting neighboring areas of the city from becoming poisoned by its effects. This urban policy of isolation and control was not unique to Shreveport and New Orleans; it was one that many cities across the United States replicated. It was a design that served to clean up the city, as well as enrich the city through a lawful revenue stream. Through the use of a registration process, houses of prostitution submitted to strict regulation, and in the process, the city assumed a paternal posture by making sure that girls employed as prostitutes were of the proper legal age. In many places across the nation (including some houses in Shreveport) women had to have a background of previous prostitution before being registered and licensed to operate. The model was not foolproof, however, Even the best efforts did nothing to consistently regulate "streetwalkers" who might not be affiliated with a licensed brothel.[202]

Within this complex economic and political environment of turn-of-the-century Shreveport, one woman in particular emerges as the prototypical businesswoman of the era's illicit culture. Annie McCune has an iconic place

The 400 Block of Milam Street in 1915. *Archives and Special Collections, Noel Memorial Library, Louisiana State University in Shreveport.*

Riverfront view of Shreveport, undated but believed to be during the 1908 flood. *Archives and Special Collections, Noel Memorial Library, Louisiana State University in Shreveport.*

all others."[199] The location did not represent the city's best real estate, and the low-lying "bottoms" were far enough removed from the river to lack the benefit of breezes in the summer. Furthermore, the land was muddy and collected water, providing a prime breeding spot for mosquitoes. However, in response to the city ordinance, prostitutes, madams and pimps all began the process of relocating their businesses.

A local newspaper story from the time of the ordinance explained the logic behind the creation of the boundaries: "As nearly as possible, the lines follow the alleys and in this way obviate the difficulty of having these houses face respectable neighborhoods. It is thought less objectionable to have an alley between the immoral and the moral."[200] This kind of "reputational segregation" isolated the less desirable elements of Shreveport society from the city's commercial prosperity and emerging upper middle class. It also served the dual purpose of removing from the public eye those politicians who transacted agreements and deals within the confines of brothels and saloons. Geographic containment of illicit behavior represented the ideal of urban reform for the era, although a different and evolving view would also bring about the end of such policies as city government itself became a target for political reformers.[201]

The Red-Light District in Shreveport

known as St. Paul's Bottoms in 1903, the area was in full economic recovery from the catastrophic downturn of the late nineteenth century and the effects of the 1873 yellow fever epidemic. In many ways, the decision of city officials to legalize the trade of prostitution can arguably be tied to the desire for continuing prosperity in the new twentieth century. Vice enforcement must have seemed especially burdensome in a river port city, where constant commerce brought in many travelers. Just as New Orleans was known for its prostitution containment in its legendary district of Storyville, so too did Shreveport develop and monitor a geographically limited district where legalized prostitution could be monitored.

The Progressive era in America that began with the turn of the new century and continued through the period of the First World War was characterized by much public debate over a variety of social issues. Not the least among these was a focus on how to deal with urban vice as cities of all sizes struggled to contend with the appropriate framework for sex, alcohol and gambling. Typically, moral reformers of the era wanted to separate and segregate the reputable businesses and classes of people from the vices of ill repute but did not seek to eradicate or eliminate the vices altogether. Interestingly, such policies of segregation to distinct areas or neighborhoods of urban areas produced social consequences long after the era of legalized prostitution passed. Eventually, progressive politicians and social reformers targeted what they saw as the exploitation of humanity at the expense of urban order and control and succeeded in eliminating legal districts of prostitution such as that which existed in Shreveport.[198]

Beginning the post–Civil War period, Shreveport followed a national pattern by attempting to legally address the issue of prostitution through a variety of ordinances that restricted the movement and activities of these women, and in 1903, a similar ordinance created the area known as St. Paul's Bottoms, named for nearby St. Paul's Methodist Church. This was a low-lying area bordered by selectively chosen streets, as well as the Texas & Pacific Railway tracks. The initial suggestion of a contained red-light district provoked some debate, as riverfront merchants may have desired the removal of brothels but simultaneously feared the resulting lack of commercial traffic. Also, brothel owners feared the loss of valuable tenants that would further isolate the riverfront area of the city. The ordinance of February 1903 allowed that "property within the prescribed limits shall constitute the red light district of the city of Shreveport to the exclusion of

The Red-Light District in Shreveport

Milam Street looking east from Marshall Street in 1911. *Archives and Special Collections, Noel Memorial Library, Louisiana State University in Shreveport.*

McCune's home was located on Cane Street (today known as Baker Street), facing toward the 900 block of Fannin Street near the edge of the district. Just across the street was the home of Nell Jester, a former schoolteacher who developed a reputation for an exclusive workforce and an even more exclusive clientele. On the opposite end of the district was the home of Bea Haywood, a lavish Victorian structure that boasted elaborate interior and exterior décor. The law of supply and demand functioned well in the area, as each madam seems to have enjoyed both comfortable personal lodgings and income.[207] Within a short time after the opening of the district, there were an estimated forty houses of prostitution in operation. At its peak, Shreveport's red-light district had over one hundred registered brothels.[208]

The region primarily attracted white clientele for white prostitutes, although there were areas in the district that featured black or "mulatto" girls, including the Octoroon Club on Fannin Street that advertised such girls from the New Orleans area. The typical rate for a "trick" was three dollars, a price that seems to have been fixed among those brothels attracting more prominent white clientele. However, there were many small-scale operators in shotgun houses who charged less than the going rate.[209] Probably first used as low-cost housing for the rapid influx of workers into the city following the

Commerce Street in 1903. *Archives and Special Collections, Noel Memorial Library, Louisiana State University in Shreveport.*

Civil War, the "shotgun house" was another important staple characteristic of the St. Paul's Bottoms area.

The prostitutes who worked for one of the prominent madams were expected to be professionals and conduct themselves with dignity and restraint. McCune and Jester were especially vigilant about the conduct and grooming of their girls, requiring them to be well mannered and schooled in etiquette and hygiene. McCune seemingly incorporated this elevated ideal of conduct for her girls with a healthy respect and understanding of the community that tolerated her enterprise. For example, McCune's girls were not allowed to shop for clothing in the same shops frequented by other women; this was done out of respect for the wives of her clients. Instead, McCune would have clothing items brought to her home so that girls could try on and select what they wanted. This is perhaps linked to McCune's reputation as a woman of influence; by observing the social codes of moral decency and restraint, she did much to attract an air of legitimacy.[210]

Just blocks from McCune's establishment were two locations that operated for blacks—those of Caesar DeBose and George Neil. These saloons inadvertently became a home for musical innovation and dance, as Neil's

The Red-Light District in Shreveport

Fannin Street looking toward the Red River in 1912. The residences are from the foreground: Doll family, Leonard Ellerbe, Will Young and Charles Selber.

venue rapidly developed more of a reputation as a rough and dangerous dance hall than a house of prostitution.[211] The area was where a blues legend came of age. Huddie William "Leadbelly" Ledbetter found his art form and made his stake to music history in the more infamous locations on Fannin Street in the first decade of the twentieth century.[212]

In a famous song by Leadbelly, "Fannin Street," the legendary artist cites his visit to the Bottoms of Shreveport and the red-light district as a sign of his coming of age at sixteen. The experiences of Leadbelly's visits to Fannin Street were formative; the music and dancing he enjoyed there left an indelible impression on him. He found that a blues style of music was popular there and soon developed his own unique sound that resonated in the black culture of the St. Paul's Bottoms. Most biographers place Leadbelly on Fannin Street as a resident among the houses of prostitution for approximately two years, although much of his life there is unknown except what can be gleaned from his own accounts.[213]

The heyday of the red-light district produced some of the richest images of Shreveport's history. It is unfortunate that due to the clandestine nature of the district and the very private lives of the women who populated those streets and buildings some of the story is lacking detail. Annie McCune is perhaps the most intriguing historical figure, yet much about her remains a mystery. There are no surviving portraits of her known to exist, and details of her private life are sketched together at best from a few public records. McCune married B.C. Secord in 1901 but then filed for divorce a year later when Secord abandoned her and left her with a diamond engagement ring that was yet to be paid for.[214] In her plot at Oakland Cemetery there is the grave of a five-year-old child named Ada Mary Carlile, born on November 16, 1895, died April 12, 1900. It is unknown if this child was Annie's or if it was the child of a prostitute she employed. There is some historical argument that the child could be Annie's, although she would have been forty-nine years old at the time the child was conceived.[215]

The lack of personal detail about the lives of the madams and prostitutes of the St. Paul's Bottoms only adds to the interest and mystique. They are women who represent a unique intersection in American history, where the practice of prostitution attracted opposite extremes of reform. It was reform-minded thinking that drove the establishment of segregated prostitution districts in the first place; it was another kind of reform mindedness that drove them out of existence. The early twentieth century allowed room for the expression of both.

As long as prostitution was a necessary social evil, its containment and control were practical courses of action. When perceptions began to shift to prostitution as a social evil linked to all others, this policy was no longer sustainable. The very concept of a red-light district increasingly came under religious and sociopolitical attack as the second decade of the twentieth century drew to a close. Social reformers from a variety of quarters began to see prostitution as something to be eradicated, along with other social ills that might be associated with it—alcohol and gambling, for example. Where the nineteenth-century prostitute had more or less been an expected fixture of frontier America, the twentieth century brought a new perspective that attacked vice and corruption of every kind. Progressivism took many forms, and the elimination of red-light districts became a focal point for many activists.[216]

Even given its history of peaceful operation, the Shreveport red-light district inevitably became entangled with all social evils of the age. It is difficult to separate the concern over the practice of prostitution itself and its associated elements of organized crime and corruption within the structures

The Red-Light District in Shreveport

of city government. By the beginning of the First World War, religious conservatives and political progressives began advocating for the elimination of legal districts of prostitution. In Shreveport, a groundswell of support for closing the district emerged from religious and civic organizations, with most major church congregations in the city taking a strong public stand. Shreveport's prostitution district no longer existed by law in November 1917, but in practice, a new era of social concern was only beginning.

In addition to the religious pressures that sought the eradication of segregated districts of prostitution, there were also profound social arguments in the public dialogue. A common assumption of the age was that no woman would become a prostitute willfully, that somehow there was an element of force or exploitation involved. This was an element that social progressives of the era could seize upon, building on the panic and paranoia of the "white slavery" investigations of the early twentieth century. Despite the convening of investigative commissions in several states, there was no conclusive evidence of the existence of large-scale organized efforts to force women into prostitution. However, the public relations damage was done by the very inquiry into the possibility, and this also contributed to the increased demand for the abolition of prostitution districts.[217] Shreveport's district was impacted by the confluence of just such religious and social reform pressures.

An abandoned red-light district is as sociologically intriguing as a vibrant and operating one. In many areas of the country, the effect of this early twentieth-century experiment in social segregation has produced dead neighborhoods full of empty and long-abandoned buildings. Because the red-light district of Shreveport, like that of many other cities, was located away from the core of the downtown business area in less-than-desirable real estate, the area has long suffered while awaiting a neighborhood renewal. Today, the area of Shreveport formerly known as St. Paul's Bottoms is known as Ledbetter Heights to honor the famous music legend known for his "Fannin Street" experiences. The historic brothels of Annie McCune and Bea Haywood are long gone. Interestingly, many residents of the area continue to refer to it by an abbreviated version of its first name. Although the designation has a topographical origin, the area's historical and cultural impact on Shreveport history continues to define what many locals simply refer to as the Bottoms.

6

The Butterfly Man: The Last Murderer Hanged in Shreveport, Louisiana

Bernadette J. Palombo, PhD

In my mind there is no doubt that this man, Fred Lockhart, is guilty and I feel as strongly as any man can feel that he should die.
—*"Message to the People from Sheriff Hughes,"* Shreveport Times, *April 18, 1934*

Much like other American cities at the turn of the twentieth century, the city of Shreveport executed convicted prisoners when local criminal courts imposed the death penalty rather than transporting them elsewhere in the state for execution as is done today. Caddo Parish prisoners today are sent to Angola State Penitentiary to await their final fates via lengthy isolation in a cell and then death administered by lethal injection. However, during the early period of the twentieth century, most death penalty convictions were carried out rather swiftly by either electrocution or hanging.

On May 18, 1934, in downtown Shreveport, at the location of the Caddo Parish Courthouse on Texas Avenue, the final official execution by hanging in the parish took place. Over the previous century, an overwhelming number of violent crimes had been committed in Shreveport.[218] Yet the death penalty case involving the rape and murder of a young female victim by the "Butterfly Man" is considered one of the most bizarre and infamous crimes—"a torture killing unparalleled for brutality in all the crime annals."[219] It was a case that gained national attention.

The Butterfly Man murder case, known more formally in legal circles as the case of the *State of Louisiana v. D.B. Napier alias Fred Lockhart* (1934), involved the torture, rape and murder of a fifteen-year-old future-bride-to-be, Miss Mae Giffin, in April 1934. An accounting of this case, covered on the front pages of daily local and regional newspapers for nearly a month, aroused the anger of the citizens of Shreveport to such magnitude that vigilante mobs, led by two women, did their best to overtake the Caddo Parish Courthouse to exact retribution and vigilante justice.[220] However, justice prevailed, and the expeditious trial and conviction of the Butterfly Man resulted in the last legal execution by hanging in the present Caddo Parish Courthouse in Shreveport, just one month after the heinous crimes had been committed.

Fred Lockhart, whose official name was Daniel Bryan "Bunce" Napier, was a thirty-eight-year-old drifter and transient who had been living with his common-law wife, Armor Anderson, in a makeshift shanty in Shreveport since the summer of 1933, less than a year before the Mae Giffin murder. Lockhart's shanty, personally constructed by Lockhart from stray bits of lumber, had a dirt floor and a cardboard partition separating the bedroom from the rest of the shack. It was only one of many such shelters in an area close to Lakeshore Drive known as "Hobo Jungle" that housed a community of poverty-stricken vagabonds.

Fred Lockhart, the "Butterfly Man." *Archives and Special Collections, Noel Memorial Library, Louisiana State University in Shreveport.*

While living in Shreveport for the previous nine months, Lockhart had attempted to make a living by selling trinkets and handmade artificial papier-mâché butterflies, some of which were known to hang on Mae Giffin's bedroom walls. The butterflies featured a clothespin design with glitter and painted wings, and Lockhart sold them door-to-door through the Queensborough section of Shreveport. It is likely

The Butterfly Man: The Last Murderer Hanged in Shreveport, Louisiana

that Lockhart sold Mae Giffin the butterflies hanging in her bedroom, and that is how he first spotted his victim.

According to one of his Hobo Jungle neighbors, Lockhart had a reputation of being "brutal, not crazy."[221] As a younger man in Georgia, Lockhart, aka Napier, had admitted to being the driver for the lynch mob that killed Leo Frank, who had been condemned to die for the murder of a young girl named Mary Fagan in 1914. Mary had been "slain in an almost identical manner as the Giffin girl," and Frank had been given the death penalty. However, when Georgia governor John Marshall Slaton changed Frank's sentence to life imprisonment, Lockhart and a group of men seized Frank from the Georgia State Prison at Milledgeville. The vigilantes then drove Frank over one hundred miles to Marietta, Georgia, to hang him near the grave of Mary Fagan. At that time, Lockhart had not been a suspect in that murder.[222]

Little is known about the early life of Fred Lockhart, except that he was originally from Macon, Georgia, and had been arrested several times for murder, rape and attempted murder. When Lockhart had been convicted of the rape and murder of a young girl in Georgia in 1926, his uncle, the former attorney general of Georgia, helped him escape the death sentence and life imprisonment for his crimes.[223] Afterward, while working on a Georgia chain gang, Lockhart escaped from a Georgia prison in the summer of 1931.[224] Lockhart briefly settled in Monroe, but after being held by the Monroe police in August 1932 for "being a fugitive from a Georgia chain gang," he was released by Monroe law enforcement when Georgia police officers refused to travel to Monroe.[225] For a brief period of time before moving to Shreveport, Lockhart resided in the small town of Ferriday, Louisiana, with his common-law wife, Armor. Lockhart was known to have been abusive to her on several occasions. In August 1933, before Lockhart and Anderson moved to Shreveport, Anderson's eighteen-year-old son, Ligon Jackson, was slain near Ferriday, with his throat cut in a manner similar to or "in almost the same manner as that of" Mae Giffin.[226] Lockhart kept a photo of his slain stepson in his Shreveport shanty, a photo that he was known to have shown to at least one visitor. The photo showed the young man's battered head and cut throat. Lockhart had previously denied any involvement in the murder of his stepson.[227] Lockhart also denied previous murders, including the hanging of Leo Frank and the 1926 murder of the young Georgia girl. He initially denied the murder of Mae Giffin in Shreveport.

Mae Giffin with her fiancé, Lee Looney. *Archives and Special Collections, Noel Memorial Library, Louisiana State University in Shreveport.*

Mae Giffin, the fifteen-year-old Shreveport victim, was deceptively lured from her mother's house on Lyba Street on Thursday, April 12, 1934. A man identifying himself as Mr. Jackson (later determined to be Lockhart) approached her at her home and offered a false promise of employment. Mae's mother, Maggie Peters, originally refused to permit her daughter to depart with him, but after much coercion, Maggie allowed the man to escort Mae to what they believed was his house at 228 Alabama Avenue. Since Mae was anxiously preparing for her future wedding and wanted to earn money to help pay for some of the expenses, she agreed to temporarily assist in housekeeping chores.

Mae Giffin did not return home on the evening of April 12. The following day, Maggie Peters went in search of her daughter at the address that Mr. Jackson (Lockhart) had given her on Alabama Street. However, Mrs. Peters discovered that the address on Alabama Avenue did not exist and that a man by the name of Mr. Jackson did not work at the streetcar barn as he had told her in their previous conversation. She immediately contacted Shreveport authorities and requested that both the police and juvenile court authorities search for her missing daughter.[228]

The Butterfly Man: The Last Murderer Hanged in Shreveport, Louisiana

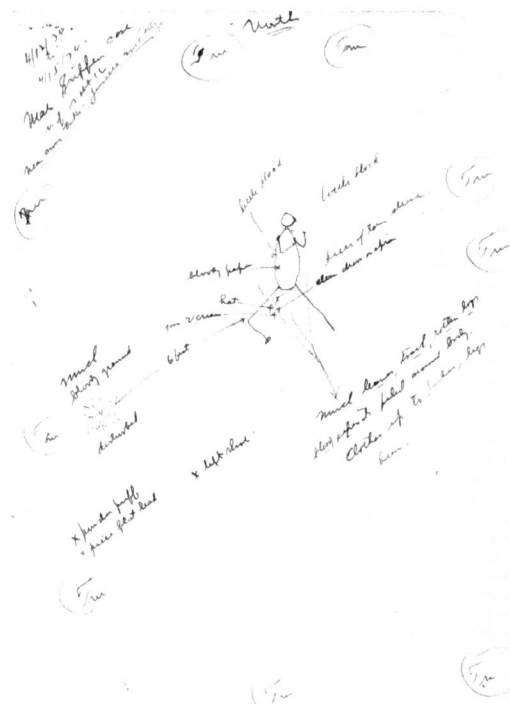

A crime scene sketch of the Mae Giffin murder scene. *Caddo Parish coroner's file. Archives and Special Collections, Noel Memorial Library, Louisiana State University in Shreveport.*

On Sunday morning, April 15, the mutilated and partially burned and decomposed body of a young female was discovered about 8:30 a.m. by two local fisherman as they were crossing through a wooded area near Cross Lake. Will Marion and Albert Green rushed to Thompson's Boat Landing and contacted the Caddo Parish Sheriff's Department to report the finding. Marion waited at the boat landing for approximately two hours until Caddo Parish sheriff Thomas Hughes, Coroner Dr. Willis P. Butler and a representative from the Wellman Undertaking Company arrived to meet him. Marion escorted the three men to the site of the victim's body.[229]

After evidence from the crime scene was preserved, the victim's body was removed from the scene and delivered to the parish morgue. The ensuing autopsy revealed numerous knife puncture wounds to the neck, side and abdomen (puncturing the liver) and upper inner thighs, as well as vaginal trauma indicating rape. The official cause of death was determined to be "traumatism by cutting, homicide."[230] The victim was identified as the missing young female, Mae Giffin, and the coroner's estimated time of death was determined to be Thursday, April 12, 1934.

Interviews with family members and neighbors following the discovery of Mae Giffin's mutilated body revealed that the man they had recognized with Miss Giffin on that date was the local man who sold handmade papier-mâché butterflies in Shreveport. Various witnesses described him as a tall, slender man with brown hair, slouching shoulders and a "hatchet face." A search was begun for the "Butterfly Man," originally identified by authorities as Fred Lockhart. However, before authorities were able to locate Lockhart, two locals also known as butterfly men, J.A. Conroy and R.J. Jackson, were arrested as suspects in Mae Giffin's murder. Initially, Mrs. Peters mistakenly identified Conroy as the man who took away her daughter the day she disappeared.[231]

Shreveport police chief Dennie Deere Blazer admitted that J.A. Conroy fit the description of the attacker. However, evidence found near the body made

Police with evidence from the May Giffin murder. *Archives and Special Collections, Noel Memorial Library, Louisiana State University in Shreveport.*

The Butterfly Man: The Last Murderer Hanged in Shreveport, Louisiana

Lockhart the primary suspect in Mae's murder. A knife found at the scene was identified by Lockhart's neighbor in the Hobo Jungle, L.H. Kelly, as a knife belonging to Fred Lockhart. Kelly not only identified the knife but also was able to tell investigators that he had borrowed the knife from Lockhart and "used it one day and broke a little dent out of the blade." Lockhart was angry about the dent Kelly had made, but he filed the knife down, "getting it razor sharp."[232] A two-day manhunt by Shreveport and Caddo Parish law enforcement officers ended on a deserted road near Tallulah, Louisiana, on Monday, April 16. L.K. Barney, chief probation officer of the Juvenile Court, and Lloyd Napier, special officer on Cross Lake, captured Fred Lockhart and returned him to Shreveport. He was booked into the Caddo Parish jail for the murder of Mae Giffin.[233]

Lockhart maintained his innocence. He insisted to authorities that he was in Jonesboro on the day of the crimes, claiming he had spent the night with a farmer (whose name he could not provide) about four miles from Ruston. Lockhart also insisted that he had joined his common-law wife in Jonesboro the next day, and from there they traveled to Tallulah, where he was captured.[234]

Once Lockhart was in custody, Caddo Parish district attorney James Galloway questioned him. However, Lockhart maintained his alibi regarding his whereabouts on Thursday, April 12, although he was not able to provide the names of the farmer or other people with whom he claimed to have stayed. Additionally, Lockhart's alibi was seriously challenged by a number of witnesses, who reported that they had seen him in the general area of Greenwood Road and Lakeshore Drive, near the crime scene on the date the crime occurred. Most incriminating was a statement by one of Lockhart's neighbors, who insisted that he saw Lockhart leave his shanty on the day of the murder after packing and departing with two suitcases.[235]

On the morning of April 17, Chief Bazer, together with five detectives from the Shreveport Police Department, returned to Lockhart's shanty to search for the clothing worn by the killer. "The officers practically destroyed the former dwelling of the slayer and his wife. They even dug under the earthen floor, hopeful of finding the garments."[236] The detectives' search of the septic tank turned up a pair of bloodstained overalls and additional articles of bloodstained clothing they believed to have been worn by Lockhart during Mae Giffin's rape and murder.

On the evening of Tuesday, April 17, 1934, Fred Lockhart confessed to authorities that on April 12 he had raped and murdered Mae Giffin in a wooded area near Cross Lake. Lockhart signed a two-page typed statement in which he confessed to local authorities that he had lured her away from her home on Alba Street with a promise of employment; he then raped and murdered her. Lockhart confessed to authorities:

> *I told her mother I wanted to hire her, and she did not want to go. I went back after that, and she said yes she would go. We went down the road… and there was a little dim road that led off to the lake. I told her my wife was down there fishing, and we would wait for her. She sat down, and I put my arms around her, and she hit me. I then asked her a question. I asked her to have intercourse with me, and she said no, and I tried anyway, then she hit me and I stabbed her in the side. I went on and had the intercourse with her, and then I cut her throat and left and went home, watered my garden and went over to Bossier City.*

He then provided details of his whereabouts before his capture near Tallulah on Monday, April 16. Lockhart's confession was printed verbatim, although the word "intercourse" was censored by both local newspapers.[237]

It was not surprising to authorities that the news of Lockhart's confession "created a wave of indignation" after it was published in the local newspapers, resulting in an angry mob headed by two young women and a local barber storming into the courthouse in an unsuccessful attempt to lynch Lockhart.[238] It was reported that the two young women "shrieked that the mob was yellow" if it did not go in with them.[239]

According to the *Shreveport Journal*, "The crowd was variously estimated at between 4,000 and 5,000, but only about two hundred…formed the actual mob…gathering about the courthouse square shortly after the *Shreveport Journal* with an extra edition, early Tuesday night [April 17] spread the news of the murderer's confession."[240]

The ferocity of the mob was apparent in news accounts: "In addition to battering down doors in the lobby, the mobsters damaged the floor considerably by dragging in a 15-foot rail and dropping it. Officers fought off the trespassers with an additional barrage of gas and seized the rail."[241] Additionally, news articles pointed to the use of tear gas as "the most effective weapon used by authorities Tuesday night in pushing back a determined mob from the courthouse. Where streams of water pumped through fire hose and sprinklers on the lawn offered only a temporary

The Butterfly Man: The Last Murderer Hanged in Shreveport, Louisiana

The courthouse was stormed by a crowd before being dispersed by the Louisiana National Guard using tear gas. *Archives and Special Collections, Noel Memorial Library, Louisiana State University in Shreveport.*

defense against the forces seeking entry to the building, the gas fumes caused a hasty retreat on all sides."[242]

When Caddo authorities exhausted their supply of tear gas by 11:00 p.m., they requested and obtained additional resources and tear gas bombs from Bossier Parish. The supplementary tear gas bombs were ignited in the building's lobby and outside the courthouse on all sides. "They effectively discouraged further entry into the courthouse lobby until the militia arrived to take charge."[243]

The following day, downtown was described as "tranquil" while four companies of the 156th Louisiana National Guard patrolled the grounds of the courthouse. Troops from Shreveport, Ruston, Minden and Monroe were stationed at all entrances of the Caddo Parish Courthouse Wednesday morning; a detail of guards walked tours in and around the lawn, and city policemen were stationed at the four corners of the square. The troops remained on duty until relieved by Governor O.K. Allen.[244]

On Wednesday morning, April 18, Judge Robert Roberts of the Caddo District Court issued a call for a special session of the parish grand jury

Second Battalion, 156th Infantry Regiment, Louisiana National Guard, in formation guarding the Caddo Parish Courthouse. *Archives and Special Collections, Noel Memorial Library, Louisiana State University in Shreveport.*

to meet on Friday, April 20, and consider the case against Lockhart.[245] On Thursday, April 19, the man known as Fred Lockhart confessed to authorities that his real name was D.B. Napier. The Butterfly Man further confessed to Sheriff Hughes that in August 1931, he had escaped from a Georgia prison while serving a life sentence for raping a girl in Crisp County, Georgia, in 1926. Lockhart, however, denied that he was guilty of the crime for which he had been convicted.[246]

Lockhart also told authorities that he was the car driver for the lynch mob that hanged Leo Frank in 1914. "Nineteen years ago, a youth named D.B. [Bruce] Napier was behind the wheel of an automobile…and in that car was Leo Frank, murderer of Mary Fagan, en route to his death at the hands of a silent, but determined band of men." The local newspaper described the Frank case as "a national sensation nearly two decades ago."[247]

The similarities between the insurrection of the Frank and Lockhart cases are remarkable. Leo Frank was convicted of murdering a child, "who was slain in an almost identical matter as the Giffin girl," and was sentenced to death. When Leo Frank's sentence was changed to life in prison by the governor of Georgia, a group of men, including Lockhart, seized the prisoner and drove 110 miles to Marietta, Georgia, where Frank was hanged near the grave of Mary Fagan.[248]

On Friday, April 20, former Caddo Parish district attorneys W.A Mabry and L.C. Blanchard were appointed as Lockhart's defense attorneys at a special session of the grand jury. He was indicted on charges of murder and rape. When the clerk of court asked Lockhart how he wished to plea to the charge of murder, Lockhart replied, "Guilty." However, District Attorney Galloway "objected to the guilty plea and at his request Judge Roberts ordered a plea of not guilty entered." The same procedure was followed on the charges of rape. According to Louisiana law at the time, the prosecution could not demand the death penalty if the accused entered a plea of guilty. The trial was set for the following Monday, April 23.[249] Judge Roberts also announced that they would return on April 30 to form an the "inquisitorial body," which would "investigate the mob violence which asserted itself last Tuesday night in an effort to wrest Lockhart from parish officers."[250]

By 9:00 a.m. on Monday April 23, family members and reporters occupied every seat in the courtroom. Spectators were allowed on a first-come, first-served basis. Members of the National Guard marched through the aisles and blocked all entrances as a preventive measure against any possible uprising. Machine guns were mounted in the lobby, while special "gas squads" stood nearby for use in the first line of defense.[251]

When the court was called to order at 10:00 a.m., Judge Roberts made a brief statement: "Conditions under which this case is being tried are well known. It has been necessary to have troops here in order to give the defendant an orderly trial. In view of last Tuesday's demonstration, we cannot afford to take any unreasonable chance on disorder in the courtroom."[252]

As jury selection began, District Attorney Galloway questioned prospective jurors about their knowledge of the case, whether they had a fixed opinion in the case and about their belief in capital punishment. L.C. Blanchard, defense counsel, listened to the prosecution's questions and accepted that the accused would receive a fair trial without any lengthy questioning of the prospective jury. By 10:55 a.m., jury selection was complete and consisted of twelve men.[253]

After the selection of the jury, District Attorney Galloway announced that he was ready for trial and made a short opening statement to the jury. He began by detailing the step-by-step events, beginning with Lockhart's first appearance at Mae Giffin's home and ending with Lockhart's confession to Caddo Parish authorities. Defense counsel did not elect to make any opening statement, and the introduction of evidence was begun. Dr. Willis P. Butler, Caddo Parish coroner, was the first witness called to the stand. Dr. Butler told of viewing the body at the crime scene and his findings from the autopsy. Dr. Butler stated that autopsy findings revealed that the girl's death was from hemorrhaging caused by stab wounds in the right side penetrating the liver. Dr. Butler presented his belief that the girl was already dead when her throat was cut, since there was only a small amount of blood from the throat wound.[254]

When the victim's mother, Mrs. Peters, was called to testify, District Attorney Galloway asked her to identify the man who had lured her daughter away on the pretext of employment. "That's the man," she said as she pointed her finger at Fred Lockhart. Mrs. Peters then apologized for mistakenly identifying J.A. Conroy on April 15 as the man who had left with her daughter. Defense counsel did not elect to cross-examine Mrs. Peters.[255]

The next witness was Sheriff Thomas Hughes, who gave a detailed description of trailing Lockhart on charges of kidnapping after Mrs. Peters first notified the Sheriff's Department of her daughter's disappearance. The sheriff then told the jury about Lockhart's confession. Sheriff Hughes stated that after he checked out Lockhart's false alibi, he told the prisoner that he had obtained strong evidence that Lockhart had lied about his whereabouts. "Lockhart said, 'You don't have to show me any evidence. I'm guilty as hell,'" testified the sheriff. The sheriff stated that Lockhart then gave a detailed confession in the presence of him, the district attorney, Police Chief Blazer and others. This confession was taken down by Miss Velda Skinner, secretary to District Attorney Galloway, and signed by Lockhart without coercion.[256] Sheriff Hughes was questioned closely by both the prosecution and the defense attorneys about whether Lockhart's confession was obtained voluntarily. The sheriff testified that no promises, threats or rewards were offered to Lockhart, ensuring the legality of Lockhart's confession to Mae Giffin's rape and murder.[257]

After Sheriff Hughes's testimony, Mrs. Furstonburg was called to the stand to tell the court about the bloodstained knife she found near the crime scene a few hours after the body was discovered. She stated that she immediately turned the knife over to Chief Blazer. The bloodstained knife was then shown to the jury. Mrs. Furstonburg was not cross-examined by the defense.[258] Chief Blazer also identified the knife found by Mrs. Furstonburg and related details of finding bloody clothing behind Lockhart's house.[259]

Leslie Y. Barnette, deputy clerk in Caddo Parish District Court, was the last witness called to testify. Mr. Barnette was present at the defendant's confession and was one of the witnesses who signed the stenographic copy of the confession. He declared that no force was used in securing the confession, and no promises had been made to the defendant.[260] The State of Louisiana rested its case after the testimony of Mr. Barnette. W.A. Mabry announced that the defense also rested its case. The defense did not call any witnesses or introduce any evidence. Lockhart chose not to take the stand, invoking his Fifth Amendment right against self-incrimination.[261] District Attorney Galloway then began his closing arguments. After stressing the seriousness of the crime, he then briefly reviewed the state's evidence and concluded with a plea for the death penalty. "This case is one of the extreme of extremes," Galloway said. "One wherein the law and evidence demand the extreme penalty."[262]

Mr. Mabry then began closing arguments for the defense. Mabry explained to the jury how he and Mr. Blanchard were chosen to defend the accused as part of their duty as members of the bar. Mr. Blanchard then summed up the defense argument in one sentence: "Gentlemen of the jury, all that I ask is that you do justice both by the State and by the defendant."[263]

Judge Roberts delivered the charge to the jury at 1:13 p.m. The twelve jurors were escorted out of the jury box by the sheriff and returned just five minutes later with their verdict. The clerk of court then read the jury's verdict: "We the jury find the defendant guilty as charged, [signed] L.H. Mitchell, Foreman." Judge Roberts then told Lockhart to stand and raise his right hand to accept his sentence. Judge Roberts declared, "It is the judgment of the court, that you, D.B. Napier, alias Fred Lockhart, be returned to the parish jail from whence you came, to remain there until such day and hour as shall be fixed by the Governor of this State, when you shall be taken hence by the Sheriff or his deputy, and hanged by the neck until you are dead, and may God have mercy on your soul."[264]

The judge and district attorney asked Governor O.K. Allen to set the execution date for Friday, April 27. The governor declined this date, stating that "swift justice had been meted out" and that fears that Lockhart "might escape just punishment had been dissipated." Governor Allen set Friday, May 18, 1934, as the execution date. No appeal from the death penalty was possible for Lockhart, as no bills of exception were reserved by his defense attorneys.[265]

At 12:09 p.m. on Friday, May 18, 1934, D.B. Napier, alias Fred Lockhart, was placed into the death trap on the seventh floor of the Caddo Parish Courthouse. Lockhart spoke to the small group of witnesses: "I want to thank the people of this state for carrying out the good old laws. This is one of the best states I've ever been in on my travels. I'm happy." The trap was released at 12:13 p.m., and at 12:26 p.m., Coroner Butler pronounced the Butterfly Man dead. Lockhart was the seventh and final person legally hanged in Caddo Parish.[266] However, he was not the last to be executed at the parish courthouse. For a short time afterward, condemned prisoners sentenced to death locally were electrocuted on the seventh floor of the courthouse in the state's traveling electric chair.[267]

Only thirty-six days separated the rape and brutal murder of fifteen-year-old victim Mae Giffin and the conviction and execution of Fred Lockhart. After his execution, Lockhart was quickly buried in the paupers' section of Greenwood Cemetery, where he rests today. The furor of Lockhart's crime subsided, and public attention quickly turned when, within a few days of Lockhart's execution, the notorious outlaws Bonnie and Clyde were seen dining and shopping in Shreveport. Five days after Lockhart's execution, Bonnie and Clyde were ambushed and shot to death in a rural area not far from town.

7

Crime of the Great Depression: The Era of Bonnie and Clyde

Cheryl H. White, PhD

> *Some day, they'll go down together.*
> *They'll bury them side by side.*
> *To a few, it'll be grief,*
> *To the law, a relief,*
> *But it's death for Bonnie and Clyde.*
> —Bonnie Parker, "The Ballad of Bonnie and Clyde"

DEPRESSION-ERA CRIME

Scholars have often cited the widespread economic hardships of the Great Depression as a primary cause of a precipitous surge in crime rates, particularly armed robbery, during the 1930s in American history. This is particularly true of a specific period usually restricted to 1932 to 1934, during which time armed robbery rates climbed to record levels in an area of the central United States that quickly became known as "the crime corridor." By the time newspaper headlines were reporting the high-profile exploits of the infamous Bonnie and Clyde, the crime wave was actually drawing near its end. In fact, the Great Depression is almost too simple an explanation, given the fact that the major rise in America's armed robberies and related crimes reached its peak in the preceding decade of the 1920s, before the collapse of the U.S. stock market.[268]

However, some social scientists insist that the most notorious 1930s criminal activity is directly attributable to the nation's profound economic woes. Certainly, it can be said that for people feeling the acute collapse of the banking and business system, the tale of Bonnie and Clyde took on the tone of a general public admiration, at least in its early stages. This is especially likely since many blamed the economic crisis on the abuses of a privileged class.[269] Clyde Barrow and Bonnie Parker represented a willingness to strike back at the nation through crime sprees, the widely reported accounts of which elevated the pair to iconic superhero status. The ability of the pair to successfully elude law enforcement authorities further cemented this image. Of course, the events surrounding their violent deaths, side by side on a barren rural road in north Louisiana, doubtlessly contributed much to their place in legend.

While the root causes of the widespread crime phenomenon of the 1920s and 1930s may be the subject of disagreement, the fact remains that it occurred precisely during a time in history when great advances occurred in firearms technology and transportation. These rapid developments played a major factor in escalating crime rates, as newer weaponry and faster transportation made possible the stereotypical "getaway" robbery. Another important factor rested with the lack of a federal structure to deal with such crime; law enforcement officials were limited to local or regional jurisdictions only. This created a scenario that played out perfectly in the decade of the 1920s in the press and in popular culture as the classic outlaw tale set in a new century. America embraced a new version of a romanticized gunslinger known as "the public enemy."[270]

Contemporary popular culture did much to promote and glorify the image of a criminal celebrity hero. For instance, the most popular genre of motion pictures in the early 1930s was the gangster film, apparently because it reflected an American culture dominated by crime and daily news reports of crime. Statistics indicate an overall 30 percent increase in the homicide rate from the decade of the 1920s to the 1930s, a figure that surely reflects the influence of Prohibition-era organized crime as well. The American moviegoer related to gangster films because they portrayed exciting characters and represented a form of escapism. Also, the film characters took on the established order and enriched themselves in the process. Interestingly, by 1934, Hollywood slowed the production of these type films and turned instead to projects that promoted a law-abiding citizenry and

Crime of the Great Depression: The Era of Bonnie and Clyde

core traditional moral values.[271] This period coincides with the deaths of some of the most famous criminal figures of the time: John Dillinger, Pretty Boy Floyd and Bonnie and Clyde, all of whom were gunned down in 1934.

It was against this unique American cultural backdrop that the notorious crime figures of Bonnie and Clyde appeared. It was indeed the era in which they belonged, and they can only be properly understood in this historical framework. The early twenty-first century does not have a cultural context for the celebrity criminal element that they represented—famous to a public that was simultaneously fascinated and horrified by their lawlessness. The era came to an end primarily because of a shift in attitudes about the nature and causes of crime, attitudes that can be traced to an emerging national response to economic hardships. By the decade of the 1930s, the public no longer romanticized the celebrity criminal because Americans began to see lawlessness as a symptom of a greater collapse at all levels of society.[272] In this way, the great crime wave of the early 1930s began to personify the economic ills of the Great Depression. So while scholars cannot simplify the Bonnie and Clyde story by blaming their criminal actions on the Great Depression, those economic conditions are perhaps responsible for bringing the era of the "public enemy" to an end.

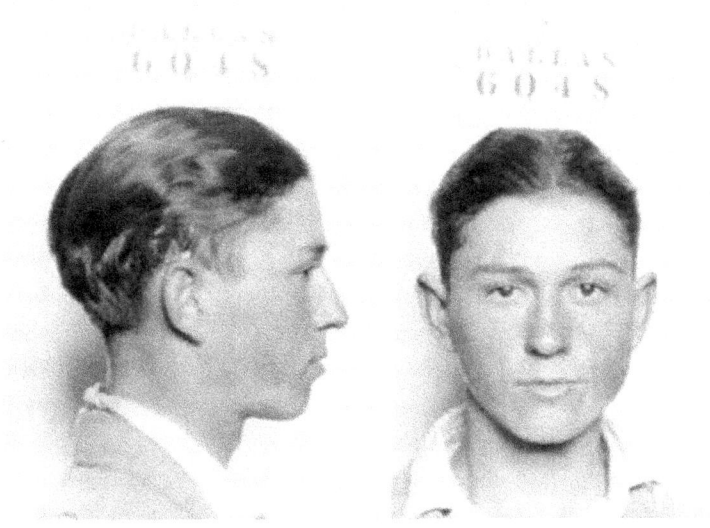

Mug shot of Clyde Barrow from Dallas, Texas, in 1932. *Courtesy Federal Bureau of Investigation.*

The Role of Shreveport and North Louisiana

The city of Shreveport mirrored all of these national attitudes and exemplified the Depression-era culture but with an economy that perhaps fared better than most. Many areas throughout the South had not yet fully recovered from the Civil War, although Shreveport continued to function vitally as a crossroads for commerce in the early twentieth century. In Louisiana, it was also the era of Huey P. Long, whose controversial approaches to public policy drove much of the economic engine of the state during his governorship from 1928 to 1932. The construction of Barksdale Air Force Base beginning in 1931 also contributed to a more stable local economic environment, and north Louisiana in general survived better than other areas of the South. However, the Shreveport community doubtlessly followed the exploits of the public enemies of the day, and the infamous tale of Bonnie and Clyde hit rather close to home.

Although Bonnie and Clyde did not commit any violent crimes in Shreveport, their story touches Shreveport history in several ways. As the closest city to the site of the pair's last days, Shreveport appears in all major crime reports and published chronicles. The *Shreveport Times* frequently reported updates on the duo's activity and suspected presence in the region, including a front-page story that appeared just six weeks before the fatal ambush that cited the "shoot to kill" order in force for the duo. In the final months of his life, Clyde Barrow stole an automobile from a Shreveport businessman and used it in the murder of two Texas law enforcement officers. In April 1934, the car was found in Kansas, and authorities were able to link it directly to Barrow through fingerprint evidence.[273]

Shreveport quite naturally became a focal point for organizing efforts to kill or capture Bonnie and Clyde, especially once their presence in north Louisiana became known in the spring of 1934. Just days before the ambush that killed him, Barrow was seen on Milam Street in Shreveport, near the Majestic Café. This knowledge certainly contributed to the ability of authorities to begin tracking the movements of the pair, an effort that eventually led to their end in a hail of gunfire near Gibsland.[274] Bonnie and Clyde are therefore inextricably linked to the crime history of Shreveport, even if only in a tangential way.

Theirs is a popularity that continues unabated and continues to attract visitors to the north Louisiana region. It is also a popularity clearly evidenced by the numerous books and films about their lives. Perhaps the ongoing public fascination with their story rests with its romanticized nature. In northern Louisiana, it is still possible today to encounter this history in a tangible way, among witnesses still living, oral histories of family members who were present and even in the now-worn historical marker that stands at the site of their ambush on a rural road near Gibsland, Louisiana. The fact that the pair knew their deaths were imminent only augments the drama. Bonnie Parker's last poem, "It's Death for Bonnie and Clyde," hinted eerily at their inevitable end.[275]

BONNIE AND CLYDE ENTER LOUISIANA LEGEND AND LORE

This is a crime saga that transects northern Louisiana but had its beginnings nearby in the state of Texas. Clyde Barrow and Bonnie Parker, both Texas natives, probably first met in 1930 in Dallas, where Bonnie worked as a waitress. By that time, Clyde had already accumulated a lengthy criminal record, including multiple felony counts of theft and burglary. Soon after their meeting, Barrow served a two-year sentence at Huntsville State Prison and resumed his relationship with Parker following his 1932 release.[276] After working briefly as a construction laborer, Barrow quickly returned to a life of crime with fellow thief Raymond Hamilton, often accompanied by Bonnie Parker. On April 23, 1932, their robbery pattern took a deadly turn with the murder of J.N. Bucher, a store owner in Hillsboro, Texas. This was the beginning of their rise to public enemy status, and over the course of the next two years, the pair and associated gang members were responsible for at least twelve deaths.[277]

In March 1933, the Barrow-Parker gang expanded to include Clyde's brother, Buck, who had just been released from prison, along with Buck's wife, Blanche Barrow. The gang took refuge in Joplin, Missouri, where they soon attracted the attention of local law enforcement, although apparently not because anyone recognized them but because of their loud and raucous behavior. A shootout ensued, and two law officers were killed. Because the gang fled quickly, they left behind a large number of personal possessions, including a roll of photographic film that contained many of the famous iconic photographs of the pair. The one that attracted the most attention was

Bonnie Parker posing in front of a car in 1933. *Courtesy Federal Bureau of Investigation.*

the image of Bonnie Parker, foot propped up on a car fender, brandishing a weapon and holding a cigar between her teeth. While first published in the local newspaper the *Joplin Globe*, the photographs soon appeared in newspapers all over the United States, and the cult following of the Barrow-Parker gang spread quickly.[278]

The chronology of the crime that ensued is one that shows evidence of an emboldened attitude, with ever-more-daring acts and near misses with law enforcement. In late April 1933, just two weeks following the Joplin murders, Barrow and Parker kidnapped a Ruston undertaker named H.D. Darby and a boardinghouse neighbor named Sophie Stone. The two were released in Arkansas the next day, and in a bizarre twist of history, Darby was an assisting mortician on the pair's bodies following their deaths just a year later. Clyde's brother, Buck Barrow, was killed in a shootout with Iowa law enforcement in July 1933, which also ended with Buck's wife, Blanche, being captured.[279]

The details of the Ruston kidnapping, along with the story of Bonnie and Clyde's escape from the Iowa posse by swimming a river, was reported

Crime of the Great Depression: The Era of Bonnie and Clyde

in every major American newspaper. Their legendary status only continued to grow. The unfolding drama also intensified the determination of law enforcement. To the lawmen who pursued the Barrow gang, all of the details seemed contradictory and confusing, for they appeared to act at random and indiscriminately decided to kill or not to kill. Equally as intriguing was the fact that the gang's leisurely drives throughout the central United States and Midwest in 1933 seemed to rely on small robberies, not ambitious get-rich schemes. The gang seems to have been interested only in the basic necessities of food and gasoline.[280]

This life on the road became a weary one for at least one of the Barrow gang: W.D. Jones, who became an enthusiastic informant to Texas law authorities when he was arrested in Houston in November 1933. Then, in early 1934, Bonnie and Clyde assisted in the escape of earlier gang member Raymond Hamilton from a Texas prison, an act that resulted in the death of a prison guard. The beginning of the end drew near as a dragnet closed around them. Escaping with Raymond Hamilton was a young convict named Henry Methvin, whose parents lived near Gibsland, Louisiana. The fateful trail of the gang inevitably led back to north Louisiana.[281]

The Barrow gang began what would be its last sweep through the South on a crime spree that produced quarreling and bitter divisions among the group. Within two months, only Henry Methvin remained with Bonnie and Clyde; Raymond Hamilton and Clyde Barrow fought violently after a bank robbery in Lancaster, Texas, and the two parted company.[282] Meanwhile, two determined deputies within the Dallas County Sheriff's Office had been pursuing the Barrow gang even in their off-duty time. Ted Hinton and Bob Alcorn were later joined by Texas Rangers Frank Hamer and Manny Gault. Upon learning of Methvin's presence in the Barrow gang, the officers began monitoring the Bienville Parish area and making discreet inquiries. The pressure intensified, however, with the murder of two state policemen in Grapevine, Texas, on Easter Sunday 1934 and then the murder of an Oklahoma constable a week later.[283]

The end came on May 23, 1934. According to the most popular contemporary account of events surrounding the ambush, Methvin's father negotiated a deal with authorities that would grant his son leniency in sentencing; he then managed to persuade his son to leave Bonnie and Clyde temporarily so that the ambush could be set. However, the authorities denied that the Methvins played any part in the ambush. The last of the

The ambush site in Bienville Parish, Louisiana. *Courtesy Federal Bureau of Investigation.*

published memoirs, those of Frank Hamer, seems to support the claim that the Methvin family played no part.[284]

However it occurred, vital information provided from within Bienville Parish clearly led to the knowledge that Bonnie and Clyde would be traveling that stretch of highway on the morning of May 23 in a tan Ford sedan. The iconic celebrity criminals met a bloody end in an ambush that literally riddled the pair with bullets. According to reports of the medical examiners, Bonnie and Clyde each suffered approximately fifty bullet wounds.[285] In the years that followed, the lore about Bonnie and Clyde spread as it touched new generations. One of the most popular touring attractions throughout the country has been the "death car" of Bonnie and Clyde. Displaying hundreds of bullet holes, it continues to be an object of morbid fascination for a public exposed anew to the lore and legend. After their embalming, the bodies of Bonnie and Clyde were put on public display in an Arcadia, Louisiana furniture store, and a seemingly endless line of people passed through to view them, a process that reportedly took several hours.[286] There can be no question that they were celebrities, dead or alive.

Crime of the Great Depression: The Era of Bonnie and Clyde

LEARNING FROM THE LEGEND

The fascination for the celebrity criminal and the public enemy of the 1930s hearkens back to an era in American history that had just witnessed the dramatic social changes of the Roaring Twenties, a devastating stock market crash and overwhelming economic losses. It was a period that transformed American culture through technological innovations, transportation and the increasing availability of news and information to the public. This was especially true given the expanding commercial use of radio. For many in America, the outlaws of the new twentieth century may have exemplified the romance of the Old West of recent memory, evoking nostalgia for the simple life that existed before the encumbrances of a rapidly changing era. In this way, Bonnie and Clyde somehow represented the past.

Yet it is also true that their story belongs to the early twentieth century as lawless vagabonds who lived and died legends amidst the worst economic conditions of American history. How much of their story can be linked to the Great Depression will likely continue to be the subject of scholarly debate. It is certainly true that the lore of Bonnie and Clyde provided a distraction for a public in the throes of economic distress, and their criminal deeds inspired sympathy among many quarters. However, the era seems to have ended as abruptly as it began. With the deaths of Bonnie and Clyde, John Dillinger and the likes, America turned its attention to a traditional morality, which would prove to be a needed reinforcement for the challenges of meeting global totalitarianism in the not-too-distant future.

The age of the FBI and the G-man depicted a new hero archetype for the nation. North Louisiana played a vital role in the end of this criminal era by bringing down Bonnie and Clyde in a controversial roadside ambush that offered the pair no opportunity to surrender. The swift and sudden end the nation brought to the celebrity criminal is a fitting metaphor for the stereotype of twentieth-century America.

8

Serial Killers: Rolling and Code

Bernadette J. Palombo, PhD

> *When subjects perpetrate crimes, particularly, the very, very first crimes they commit, they must commit the crimes on the home turf area; areas where they feel very, very comfortable.*
> —*FBI special agent John E. Douglas in a transcript,* State of Louisiana v. Nathaniel Code

Serial murders have made an impact on the social consciousness of all Americans. The names of serial killers are well known, and in some circles, these killers have become celebrities. Regardless of the manner in which we view serial murder, attention is reflected in the media to their crimes and others who commit such similar offenses. Serial murder remains at the apex of interest and attention.[287] Serial murderers can come from small towns and rural communities, not only from large cities and states.[288] The apprehension of serial killers by professionals in the criminal justice system appears to occur almost by accident. Due largely to the senselessness of their crimes, the often extremely brutal nature of the killings, widespread coverage of their crimes in the mainstream media, their mobility and their intelligence (or alternatively, a primal sense of cunning), they may go on for years without being apprehended.[289] One compelling fact is apparent: in contemporary times, there has appeared a class of homicidal predators who pose a clear and present danger to more than five thousand Americans yearly.[290] Certainly, this is evidence enough that the criminal justice system must take notice and develop a plan of action.[291]

National public attention became focused on several high-profile serial murder cases from the late 1960s through the 1990s. Beginning with the Sharon Tate–LaBianca family murders by the Charles Manson family in California in 1969, the public was fed a steady diet of gruesome details and courtroom drama. Several other killers caught the public's eye over the next two decades. Each seemed to strike fear in different forms. Serial murderer John Wayne Gacy killed at least thirty-two people in Illinois between 1972 and 1978. Coral Eugene Watts murdered eighty people in Michigan between 1974 and 1982. Theodore "Ted" Bundy killed perhaps as many as forty people from Washington to Florida, practicing necrophilia on the corpses, between 1974 and 1978. David Berkowitz, the publicity-seeking "Son of Sam" or ".44-Caliber Killer," murdered at least six people in New York between 1976 and 1977. Jeffrey Dalmer, a cannibal from Wisconsin, killed fifteen people between 1978 and 1991. Gary Ridgway, the "Green River Killer" from Washington, killed forty-eight people between 1982 and 1984. Richard Angelo murdered twenty-five people in Good Samaritan Hospital in Long Island, New York, between April and October 1987. In Louisiana, between the late 1960s and early 1990s, the southern part of the state experienced seventy-seven or more murders committed by thirteen serial murderers, and in the northern part of the state, Shreveport experienced twelve serial murders at the hands of two local serial murderers, Nathanial Code and Danny Rolling. No systematic method of identifying these types of cases existed until the early 1970s. Until then, work was done by hand and with, by today's standards, crude scientific instruments. The science of forensics remained in its infancy.

The Federal Bureau of Investigation began a systematic study of the science of psychological analysis of criminal behavior in 1972—what is today commonly known as "profiling."[292] Although most professionals at the time considered the new techniques developed at the FBI Academy at Quantico, Virginia, to be odd and perhaps "fake" science, time has proven psychologists, as the other professionals of the Behavioral Sciences Unit (BSU) of the National Center for Analysis of Violent Crime, to be the absolute leaders in the field.[293]

Among the stellar scholars who gravitated to the BSU was John E. Douglas, a criminal psychologist. He became, perhaps, the most famous profiler in the FBI.[294] Douglas interviewed many of the most infamous criminals of the late twentieth century as part of his research, profiling and

Serial Killers: Rolling and Code

reporting tasks. During the 1980s, John Douglas's duties at the FBI Academy and the Behavioral Science Unit involved him in two cases in northwestern Louisiana. The violent outbreak of serial murders all over the nation created the appearance that no place in America was immune. This was certainly true of Shreveport, Louisiana.

Shreveport is home to several well-established neighborhoods that date back to the nineteenth and early twentieth centuries. Among these are Cedar Grove, Mooretown and Allendale. All contain predominately African American populations. Beginning in 1984 and continuing over a three-year period, a series of horrific murders plagued these neighborhoods, particularly Cedar Grove.

Deborah Ann Ford was a twenty-five-year-old single mother of two daughters. She lived at 315 East Seventy-fourth Street. On the night of August 30, 1984, she sent her daughters to visit their grandmother and spent the night visiting friends before falling asleep on the couch in the living room. Sometime after midnight, someone pried open the screen on a window in the back of the house and entered the unlocked window.[295] The intruder saw the sleeping woman and then looked around for items that he could use. He found a box fan and cut the electrical cord from it. He found Ford's robe in another room.[296] The intruder then viciously attacked Deborah Ford. She fought back but was quickly overpowered. She had a pistol on the couch with her but never had a chance to use it. The intruder punched her until she was semiconscious or unconscious. He then hog-tied Ford, placing her hands behind her back with the electrical cord. He gagged her with the robe. The method of tying her was unique—what the FBI would later term a signature of the killer.[297] Her hands were tied in a manner that resembled handcuffs. The intruder then stabbed Ford in the chest nine times and slashed her throat six times, eventually with enough force that she was almost decapitated. He dragged Ford to the middle of the room and posed her, then wiped her blood on the sofa cushions, turned up the air conditioner and turned on the stereo to a high volume. He then stole Ford's purse and left though the same window he had entered.[298]

The intruder did not simply commit murder and robbery. This was an act of overkill, showing tremendous rage. Dr. George McCormick, the Caddo Parish coroner, examined the scene and realized that this was not a typical murder scene, if such a thing exists. He told the authorities that "the killer will strike again."[299] Dr. McCormick realized that Shreveport had a serial killer in its midst due to the ritual aspects of the murder, the intentional positioning of the body for effect, the extreme overkill and the odd method of restraining the victim.[300] There were no leads.

Cedar Grove was quiet until the following summer. Violent overkill murders occurred on St. Vincent Avenue and Ashton Street on June 24 and July 18, 1985, respectively. In both cases, Nathaniel Code Jr., a local man, was later implicated but never charged.[301] Code had been released from the Louisiana State Penitentiary at Angola on January 23, 1984 (seven months before the Ford murder), after serving eight years of a fifteen-year sentence for aggravated rape.[302]

Violent crimes continued on July 19, 1985, when four people were butchered in a house at 213 East Seventy-second Street in Cedar Grove. Vivian Chaney, thirty-seven; her fifteen-year-old daughter, Carlitha Culbert; Chaney's brother, Jerry Culbert, twenty-five; and Chaney's boyfriend, Billy Joe Harris, were murdered. Two of Chaney's daughters, ages seven and ten years old, were spared and unharmed.[303] The scene was a gruesome bloodbath, and the bodies were posed. Some of the victims were tied in the

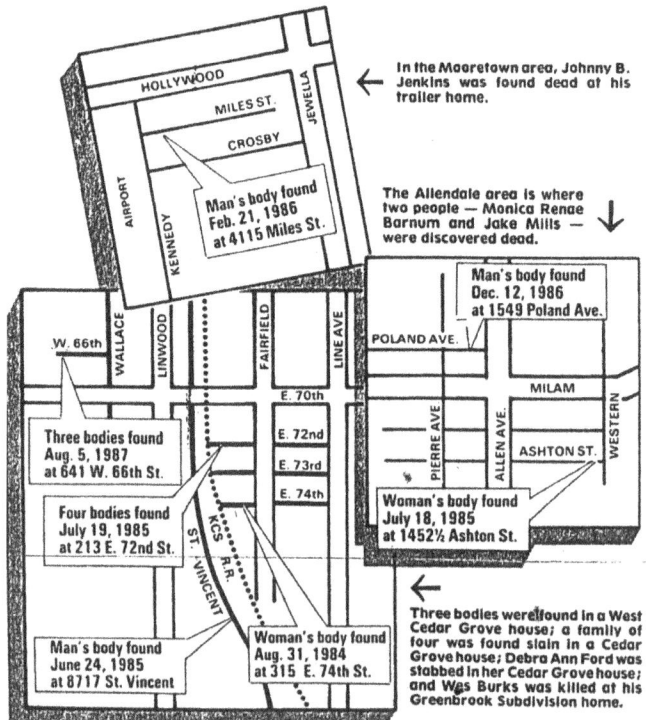

Map of the Code murders. *Courtesy* Shreveport Times, *April 7, 1987.*

Serial Killers: Rolling and Code

same fashion as Deborah Ford's had been.[304] The police described the scene as "horrific," and Dr. McCormick linked the killings to the Ford murder by style, overkill and methodology.[305]

Two more murders occurred, the first on February 21, 1986, and another on December 12, 1986. The cases were similar to the previous homicides, and Code was later listed as a suspect but never charged. Then Cedar Grove went quiet until the late summer of 1987.

William T. Code, age seventy-two, Nathaniel Code Jr.'s grandfather, and two young nephews of Nathaniel Code Jr. were brutally murdered on August 5, 1987. The crime scene was similar to the Ford and Chaney murders. Code was in the crowd when the police arrived and offered to give a statement. He was arrested the following day and charged with the first-degree murder of the four victims in the Chaney home. At that time, he was listed as a suspect in eight other homicides, including those of the previous day.[306]

The problem for prosecutors was how to link the crimes. Some victims were gagged, but not all. Some were stabbed, others strangled and the remainder shot.[307] The district attorney turned to John Douglas of the FBI's Behavioral Sciences Unit. Douglas profiled the killer and determined that although the murders differed in *modus operandi* (MO, or method of operation), he was able to identify a significant signature that bound Code to the crimes.[308] The trial lasted from September 17, 1990, until October 6, 1990. The jury deliberated for an hour before finding Nathaniel Code Jr. guilty of the four Chaney murders.[309] He was sentenced to death on October 9, 1990. Through a

Nathaniel Code under arrest in the Caddo Parish, Louisiana Courthouse. *Courtesy Mike Silva, Shreveport Times.*

long series of proceedings, Code's attorneys have delayed the execution, and at the time of this writing, Nathaniel Code still sits on death row at Angola State Penitentiary. The lead prosecutor in the case, now Caddo Parish district judge Scott Crichton, stated that Code was "no doubt one of the worst serial killers in this country and the worst criminal in the history of Caddo Parish."[310]

Shreveport's second serial murderer was Danny Harold Rolling, born in 1954, the eldest son of a retired Shreveport police lieutenant. It was alleged that Rolling's father, James Rolling, regularly abused his sons, beating Danny and his brother when they were children and teenagers, often blindfolding and binding them.[311] Danny Rolling's mother always seemed to defend her husband at the expense of her sons.[312]

Danny Rolling failed the third grade, became aggressive and suffered from an ongoing inferiority complex. When he was thirteen, Rolling's father arrested him for drinking and made certain that his son was confined to jail for two weeks. Danny then began a series of attempts to run away from home but always returned. Rolling's academic career came to a close when he failed the tenth grade and dropped out of school. He joined the U.S. Air Force but was discharged prematurely due to a psychiatric diagnosis of an unspecified personality disorder. Rolling became a chronic drug and alcohol abuser. He married in 1974 and fathered a child, but the marriage failed in 1977. Rolling became a drifter and petty criminal and headed east.[313]

Rolling bungled crimes in Georgia, Alabama and Mississippi, each time earning multiple-year sentences, and was moved from penitentiary to penitentiary within these states.[314] While on parole from the Mississippi correctional system, Rolling returned to Shreveport in 1988. He moved back to his parents' West Canal Boulevard home and exhibited bizarre behavior. The parolee dressed in camouflage pants and wore combat boots and a bandana around his head. He jogged in the neighborhood carrying a log on his shoulder. Children in the area called him "Rambo," a character Rolling was obviously mimicking.[315] He later stated that he had multiple personalities and that one, whom he called "Gemini," was evil.[316]

Early on Monday morning, November 6, 1989, a neighbor went to the home of William T. Grissom at 2011 Beth Lane in the Southern Hills neighborhood of Shreveport. The neighbor, who had been asked by William Grissom's daughter to check on him and her son, who was visiting, looked inside and immediately called police.[317] Inside the home in this quiet middle-class neighborhood were the bodies of William Grissom, fifty-five; his daughter, Julie Grissom, twenty-three; and William Grissom's grandson (and Julie Grissom's nephew), Sean, eight. All had been stabbed.[318] The violence of the crime indicated that Julie Grissom was the target and that overkill was present. Although not reported at the time, Julie Grissom had been raped, covered with bite marks, slashed in the back and mutilated. Her body had been washed down in soap and vinegar to destroy evidence and then posed in a sexually suggestive position on the edge of the bed, with her legs spread to shock whoever found her.[319]

The police knew they had a mass murderer, if not a serial killer, loose on the streets of Shreveport. There were no leads. The following day, news reports carried the first details of the heinous crimes.[320] Dr. George McCormick, the Caddo Parish coroner, performed autopsies and told the media, "They were all purposefully killing wounds," adding that the weapon used was "a big knife."[321] The North Louisiana Criminalistics Laboratory gathered fingerprints, blood and evidence from the scene for processing.[322]

Julie Grissom. *Archives and Special Collections, Noel Memorial Library, Louisiana State University in Shreveport.*

The police were baffled with no real leads. Their investigation focused on Julie Grissom's former boyfriend, a local attorney named Hal Carter, to the exclusion of any other possible perpetrators. The Shreveport Police contacted the FBI's Behavioral Science Unit at Quantico, Virginia, and met with BSU profilers on January 8, 1990.[323] The BSU agents told the SPD officers that the UNSUB (unknown subject) was a white male in his twenties or early thirties who considered himself to be a "macho man." He would dress neatly and was of average intelligence but was a high school dropout with authority issues. He would not be remorseful for his actions. They also believed he had prior run-ins with the law and that he exhibited a high degree of criminal sophistication. They believed he changed jobs frequently. They added that the UNSUB knew Julie Grissom and had stalked her.[324] The BSU profilers were asked about Carter and how he might have accomplished the murders.[325] Carter had been out of state at the time of the murders, and although he did not meet the BSU profile of the UNSUB, that did not deter the detectives. Carter eventually sued the City of Shreveport and the *Shreveport Times* for his mistreatment and harassment.[326]

Danny Rolling during his sentencing hearing. *Associated Press Photo.*

Serial Killers: Rolling and Code

Danny Rolling got into a fight with his father on May 17, 1990, over who should roll up a car window while it rained. Danny shot his father in the head but did not kill him. Danny then fled the state and went to Gainesville, Florida.[327] A warrant was issued for Rolling's arrest for the attempted murder of his father.

Gainesville, Florida, saw five murders in three days in August 1990. Four young female students and a male roommate of one of them were found stabbed and mutilated, and in some cases, the bodies were washed in peroxide to destroy evidence. The University of Florida and the surrounding community was in panic. Shreveporter Danny Rolling burglarized some homes and tried to rob a bank on September 1, 1990, but was caught.[328] He sat in jail while the murders were investigated. Eventually, the Florida investigators found a link between Rolling and the Grissom murders and contacted the Shreveport Police Department for information on his activities in Louisiana.[329] The SPD did not readily cooperate. It was still focused on Shreveport attorney Hal Carter for these horrible crimes.[330]

Finally, DNA evidence linked the cases in Florida to Rolling, but Shreveport police could not easily connect him to the Grissom murders. Rolling was tried and convicted of the Florida burglaries. When the murder trials began, Rolling pleaded guilty and was sentenced to die on April 20, 1994. While he hoped to be spared execution in Florida, Danny Rolling made a long, rambling confession to his fiancée, admitting to the Grissom murders. He was extraordinarily explicit in his account. There can be no doubt that Rolling was the murderer.[331] Danny Rolling was executed by the State of Florida via lethal injection at the Starke Penitentiary on October 25, 2006. Just before his execution, Rolling was asked if he had any final words. Witnesses at the execution said Rolling sang a song and repeated the line "None greater than thee, oh Lord."[332]

These are but two of the most brutal serial murderers identified in the United States. The decades since the 1960s have seen a huge increase in this form of predator, and the FBI's Behavioral Science Unit has gained tremendous attention in its expertise in profiling these monsters who live among us. Ronald M. Holmes and Stephen T. Holmes, in their book *Serial Murder*, give a chilling estimate of the number of serial killers active in the United States today. They state, "The U.S. Department of Justice at one time estimated that as many as 35 serial killers were roaming the streets and towns of the United States...From our contacts with law enforcement officials all over

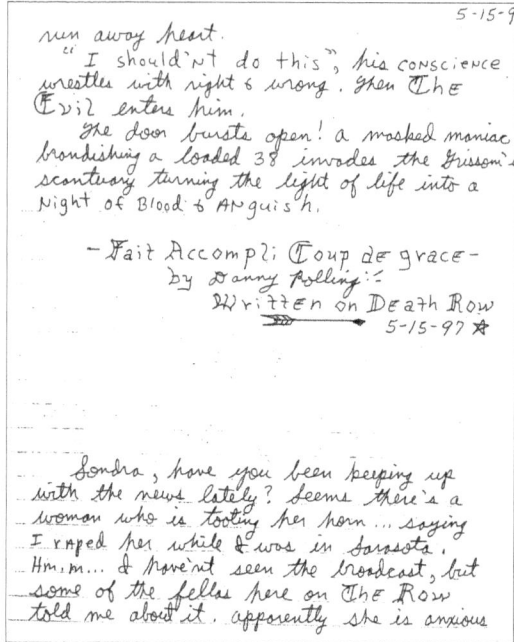

A page from Danny Rolling's diary describing the death of Julie Grissom. *Archives and Special Collections, Noel Memorial Library, Louisiana State University in Shreveport.*

the United States, we believe that a more accurate count may be as high as 200."[333]

For all of the horror and mayhem these people have created and continue to create, there are some true heroes in this saga. John Douglas and his team at the FBI BSU unit created the first scientific methodology to study serial killers. They are the best in the world. Douglas, now retired from the FBI, continues to be very active in consulting and has authored many of the best works in the field.[334] The scientists who collect and collate the data usually work outside the glaring light of the press and public view. The professionals who keep the public safe are owed a tremendous debt of gratitude.

One such person who was "maligned" following his death was Dr. George McCormick. Dr. McCormick was a true professional who first recognized that Shreveport had a serial killer in the Nathaniel Code case; he processed hundreds of homicides over the span of twenty-three years, including the Grissom family murders committed by Danny Rolling. He was remarkably intelligent and possessed a superbly analytical mind. Dr. McCormick's institutional memory for cases and minute details associated with them made the coroner a formidable weapon in courtroom. He could be gruff and authoritarian, but his ability to analyze a crime scene and victim's body were unequalled.

Finally, the people who meet their tragic deaths at the hands of serial killers must be remembered outside their immediate families and circles of friends. Not one of them deserves the death imposed by serial killers. Their families must be considered victims as well. They truly deserve society's continued support.

Notes

Chapter 1

1. Walker, *Popular Justice*, 15.
2. Drago, *Great Range Wars*, 28.
3. For an extensive list of early settlers buried in Shreveport's Oakland Cemetery, see http://www.oaklandcemeteryla.org/Index.aspx.
4. Ruffin, "Invasion of Shreveport," 26.
5. Leonard Memoirs. Leonard wrote his memoirs in 1914. He was a law student and was selected clerk for the police jury and secretary of the city council. In 1872, Leonard became a founder and editor of the *Shreveport Times*. Annotations within the collection were made by historian Eric J. Brock in 1992.
6. U.S. Dept. of Commerce, Seventh Decennial Census (1850).
7. Leonard Memoirs, 17. David Hester filled an unexpired term in the Louisiana legislature and was not elected. The duel occurred on December 20, 1849. Hester's succession is found in Caddo Parish Probate Record No. 325. Leonard recalled the gunfight occurring during the first week he was in Shreveport. It was three months later.
8. Ibid.
9. Ibid., 15; Brock annotation. Rufus Sewall Sr.'s grave is the oldest marked grave in Oakland Cemetery.

10. Henrice, *Shreveport*, 59–60; Leonard Memoirs, Brock annotation. The duel was fought on June 20, 1842.
11. Leonard Memoirs, 32.
12. McLure and Howe, *History of Shreveport*, 292
13. Flournoy Family Papers. This collection includes a series of typewritten transcripts entitled "Writings of J.P. Flournoy, Sr." This quote is found in a typescript, "Some of the Families Who Lived in and Around Greenwood in 1859–1860."
14. This was actually the original Southern Pacific Railroad.
15. Ibid.
16. Leonard Memoirs, 38.
17. Schultz, *Quantrill's War*, 165.
18. Ibid., 269.
19. King, *No Pardons to Ask*, 124, notes 282. King's diary entry was for Thursday, November 26, 1863, reporting on events of the prior Sunday.
20. Hogue, *Uncivil War*, 4.
21. U.S. Congress, *Condition of Affairs in Late Insurrectionary States*, 21; Perman, *Pursuit of Unity*, 133.
22. *Exodus Committee*, "Negro Exodus from Southern States," xviii; Du Bois, *Black Reconstruction*, 468–69.
23. Compilation from *Shreveport Times* daily tabulations August 20–November 15, 1873, by Gary D. Joiner, with assistance by Eric J. Brock.
24. *Shreveport Times*, November 15, 1873.
25. Ibid., October 1, 1873.
26. B'nai Zion Temple cemetery records.
27. *Shreveport Times*, July 9, 1874.
28. Brock, *Brock's Shreveport*, 185.
29. Monument of Nathan Goldkind, Oakland Cemetery, Shreveport, Louisiana.
30. Brock, *Brock's Shreveport*, 184.
31. *State of Louisiana v. Gus Logan* No. 6214; *Supreme Court, State of Louisiana v. Gus Logan*, 37 LA Ann. 778, No. 165. Governor McEnery's commutation attached to file; Brock, *Brock's Shreveport*, 185.
32. *New York Times*, June 18, 1886; Brock, *Brock's Shreveport*, 185.

Chapter 2

33. *Montgomery* [Alabama] *Advertiser*, April 26, 1959.
34. Brundage, *Lynching in the New South*, 291.
35. Ibid., 17–48; http://academic.evergreen.edu/p/pfeifferm/louisiana.html.
36. Pfeiffer, *Rough Justice*, for a very thorough treatment of lynching in this time period.
37. Pfeiffer, "Lynching and Criminal Justice," 155–77.
38. Pfeiffer, *Rough Justice*, Appendix C., 161–78; http://academic.evergreen.edu/p/pfeifferm/louisiana.html.
39. See, for example, Ginzburg, *100 Years of Lynchings*; Tolnay and Beck, *Festival of Violence*; Raper, *Tragedy of Lynching*; and Brundage, *Under Sentence of Death*.
40. Joiner and Roberson, *Lost Shreveport*, 81–84.
41. From data found in Pfeiffer, *Rough Justice*, Appendix C., 161–78.
42. Slattery family papers. Personal communication with Joe Slattery, Shreveport, Louisiana, July 17, 2010. A photograph of the tree is found in O'Pry, *Chronicles of Shreveport*, 315.
43. *Shreveport Times*, November 29, 1892.
44. Ibid., July 26, 1903; *Chicago Record-Herald*, July 27, 1903.
45. *Shreveport Times*, April 9, 1912.
46. *Montgomery* [Alabama] *Advertiser*, April 10, 1912.
47. John Gray Foster Memorial Volume.
48. *Times-Picayune*, December 13, 1900
49. Map of Foster Plantation, Bossier Parish, Louisiana.
50. Probate Record of James Martin Foster Sr.
51. *New York Times*, June 14, 1901.
52. *Dallas Morning News*, June 13, 1901.
53. *New York Times*, June 13, 1901.
54. *New Orleans Item*, June 13, 1901.
55. *Columbus* [Georgia] *Daily Enquirer*, June 15, 1901; *Aurora* [Illinois] *Daily Express*, June 14, 1901; *New York Times*, June 14, 1901.
56. Ibid.
57. *Chicago Record-Herald*, June 20, 1901; *New Orleans Item*, June 21, 1901.
58. *Shreveport Journal*, June 15, 1901.
59. *Shreveport Times*, June 15, 1901.
60. *New Orleans Item*, June 15, 1901.

61. *Columbus* [Georgia] *Daily Inquirer*, June 21, 1901; *Omaha World Herald*, June 20, 1901;
62. *Chicago Record-Herald*, June 20, 1901.
63. For an extended discussion of the Coleman case, see Joiner and Roberson, *Lost Shreveport*, 81–84.
64. *Shreveport Times*, November 28, 1909.
65. Ibid.
66. Ibid.
67. *New Orleans Item*, December 17, 1909.
68. Ibid.
69. *Dallas Morning News*, January 14, 1910, *Shreveport Times*, January 14, 1910.
70. *Philadelphia Enquirer*, August 27, 1916; *Shreveport Journal*, August 26, 1916.
71. *Shreveport Times*, January 4, 1923.
72. *St. Louis Argus*, January 12, 1923.
73. *Shreveport Times*, January 4, 1923.
74. Ibid.
75. From data found in Pfeiffer, *Rough Justice*, Appendix C., 161–78
76. Ibid.

Chapter 3

77. Trelease, *White Terror*, 3.
78. Randel, *Ku Klux Klan*, 9.
79. A den was a formal meeting place for a local Klan group.
80. Randel, *Ku Klux Klan*, 13, 16.
81. Dauphine, "Knights of the White Camelia," 173.
82. Tunnell, *Crucible of Reconstruction*, 153.
83. Trelease, *White Terror*, 127.
84. Ibid., 127–28.
85. Taylor, *Louisiana Reconstructed*, 161–64.
86. Due to the development and maintenance of large cotton plantations along the Red River before the Civil War, a large number of slaves were brought in to work the fields.
87. Vandal, *Rethinking Southern Violence*, 49.
88. Ibid., 49–50.
89. Dauphine, "Knights of the White Camelia," 184–86.

90. Trelease, *White Terror*, 95.
91. Louisiana General Assembly, *Conduct of the Late Elections*, 155.
92. Vandal, "'Bloody Caddo,'" 177.
93. Tunnell, *Edge of the Sword*, 129.
94. Louisiana General Assembly, *Conduct of the Late Elections*, 16.
95. Vandal, " Policy of Violence," 174.
96. Louisiana General Assembly, *Conduct of the Late Elections*, 17.
97. Ibid., 133–35.
98. Ibid., 35.
99. Tunnell, *Edge of the Sword*, 189.
100. *Alexandria Caucasian*, April 4, 1874, quoted in Taylor, *Louisiana Reconstructed*, 281–82.
101. Taylor, *Louisiana Reconstructed*, 282.
102. Vandal, "Albert H. Leonard's Road," 60.
103. Vandal, *Rethinking Southern Violence*, 104.
104. Vandal, " Policy of Violence ," 175, 178.
105. Tunnell, *Edge of the Sword*, 289.
106. Vandal, *Rethinking Southern Violence*, 100.
107. Taylor, *Louisiana Reconstructed*, 299.
108. Trelease, *White Terror*, 136.
109. Peoples, "'Kansas Fever,'" 122.
110. Alexander, *Ku Klux Klan*, 2–8.
111. Harrell, "Ku Klux Klan in Louisiana," 113.
112. Ibid., 124–25.
113. *Shreveport Journal*, April 10, 1921.
114. Harrell, "Ku Klux Klan in Louisiana," 129.
115. Alexander, *Ku Klux Klan*, 43.
116. Ibid., 90.
117. Harrell, "Ku Klux Klan in Louisiana," 139.
118. A Konklave is any gathering, large or small, of Klansmen.
119. *Shreveport Journal*, September 15, 1923.
120. Harrell, "Ku Klux Klan in Louisiana," 180.
121 Alexander, *Ku Klux Klan*, 210–11.
122. Anti-Defamation League, "Ku Klux Klan."
123. Wade, *Fiery Cross*, 368–96.
124. Southern Poverty Law Center, "Hate Map."
125. Extremism and Radicalization Branch, *Rightwing Extremism*, 2.

Chapter 4

126. Coffey, *Long Thirst*, 5.
127. Ibid., 3.
128. Ibid., 5.
129. Ibid., 7.
130. U.S. Constitution, Amendment 18.
131. Vance, "Demise of Prohibition," 100.
132. *Times-Picayune*, January 15, 1908.
133. Ibid.
134. *Times-Picayune*, January 1, 1908.
135. Ibid.
136. Another name for a speakeasy, a blind tiger is a place where alcoholic beverages were sold illegally. Basically, proprietors would charge bar patrons a fee to see a "blind tiger" (or a "blind pig"). While there, the patrons would enjoy "complimentary" drinks. Another popular definition given by a restaurant in Shreveport with the same name suggests that restaurants offering to sell prohibited alcohol in back rooms would let patrons know by placing toy tigers on the tables. The tigers would turn a blind eye to the illegal behavior. See http://www.blindtigerrestaurant.com for further information.
137. *Times-Picayune*, January 1, 1908.
138. Ibid., January 15, 1908.
139. Ibid.
140. Jackson, "Prohibition in New Orleans," 262.
141. *Times-Picayune*, October 3, 1909.
142 Ibid.
143. *Times-Picayune*, June 17, 1910.
144. Ibid., January 31, 1911.
145. Ibid., October 22, 1911.
146. Ibid., July 8, 1912.
147. Ibid., February 10, 1913.
148. Clark, *Deliver Us From Evil*, 119.
149. A public nuisance is any property where criminal activity occurs.
150. *Times-Picayune*, March 4, 1913.
151. Ibid., April 3, 1913.
152. Ibid., July 4, 1913.

153. Ibid., June 30, 1915.
154. Ibid., April 7, 1916.
155. Adjusted for inflation, this would be an equivalent of $25,897 today.
156. *Times-Picayune*, December 20, 1915.
157. Ibid.
158. *Times-Picayune*, October 9, 1916.
159. Ibid., January 6, 1919.
160. Ibid.
161. Jackson, "Prohibition in New Orleans," 263.
162. *Times-Picayune*, October 18, 1915.
163. Adjusted for inflation, this would be an equivalent of $1,402,745 today.
164. *Times-Picayune*, October 18, 1915.
165. Ibid.
166. Stelzle, *Why Prohibition!*, 48–49.
167. Ibid.
168. Kyvig, *Repealing National Prohibition*, 10.
169. *Times-Picayune*, October 18, 1915.
170. Ibid.
171. Kyvig, *Repealing National Prohibition*, 10.
172. Ibid., 11.
173. Ibid., 11.
174. Jackson, "Prohibition in New Orleans," 263.
175. In fact, the Anti-Saloon League was extremely successful in a number of local option elections across the United States.
176. *Times-Picayune*, December 9, 1917.
177. Jackson, "Prohibition in New Orleans," 262.
178. *Times-Picayune*, August 9, 1918.
179. Ibid.
180. Kyvig, *Repealing National Prohibition*, 12.
181. *Times-Picayune*, January 16, 1920.
182. In total, close to one thousand people were killed by federal Prohibition agents, Coast Guard soldiers and state and municipal officers.
183. Vance, "Demise of Prohibition," 101 - 102.
184. Harrell, " Ku Klux Klan," 129.
185. Vance, "Demise of Prohibition," 99.
186. Kyvig, *Repealing National Prohibition*, 21.
187. Ibid., 20–21.

188. Coffey, *Long Thirst*, 316.
189. Ibid., 178.
190. Jackson, "Prohibition in New Orleans," 282.
191. Ibid., 283.
192. US Constitution, Amendment 21.

Chapter 5

193. Sanger, *History of Prostitution*, 36.
194. Stuck, *Annie McCune*, 3.
195. Woolston, *Prostitution in the United States*, 25.
196. Shreveport City Records. Proceedings of the City Council of Shreveport, 88.
197. Woolston, *Prostitution in the United States*, 26.
198. Keire, *For Business and Pleasure*, 3.
199. Stuck, *Annie McCune*, 11.
200. Ibid.
201. Mara Keire uses the term "reputational segregation" to describe the overall policies of urban reformers in the United States during the first decades of the twentieth century. It is a term that also connotes the desire for the continued existence of vice, with a corresponding need to manage it in such a way that permitted the local officials and city political machines to function within both the accepted public sphere and the illicit one.
202. Woolston, *Prostitution in the United States*, 107.
203. Stuck, *Annie McCune*, 4.
204. Ibid., 7.
205. United States Census, Year 1900.
206. Ditmore, *Encyclopedia of Prostitution*, 154.
207. Stuck, *Annie McCune*, 12–13.
208. Laird and Lornell, *Shreveport Sounds*, 147.
209. Ibid., 147.
210. Stuck, *Annie McCune*, 22.
211. Laird and Lornell, *Shreveport Sounds*, 147–48.
212. Ibid., 140.
213. Ibid., 152.
214. Stuck, *Annie McCune*, 8.

215. Goodloe Stuck revealed that in conveyance records from the Caddo Parish Courthouse of 1888 and 1889 there is found the signature of a "Mrs. Annie Carlile" in the same handwriting as that which appears on Annie McCune's handwritten will. However, there is no record of a marriage to a man named Carlile.
216. Esselstyn, "Prostitution in the United States," 123–35.
217. Woolston, *Prostitution in the United States*, 161.

Chapter 6

218. Brock, *Brock's Shreveport*, 194.
219. *Shreveport Times*, "Torture Killer Murders Girl Here; Attempts to Burn Body," April 16, 1934.
220. Brock, *Brock's Shreveport*, 196.
221. *Shreveport Journal*, "Slayer Confesses He is a Fugitive from Georgia Pen," April 19, 1934.
222. *Shreveport Journal*, "Trial of Lockhart Monday, Speedy Justice for Man Who Killed Mac Giffin," April 19, 1934.
223 Brock, *Brock's Shreveport*, 195.
224. *Shreveport Times*, "Lockhart Says He Was Car Driver for Men Who Killed Leo Frank," April 20, 1934.
225. Ibid.
226. *Shreveport Times*, "Lockhart Confesses Girl Torture Murder," April 18, 1934.
227. *Shreveport Times*, "Neighbor of Lockhart in Hobo Jungle Describes Family Life of Man, Woman," April 18, 1934.
228. *Shreveport Times*, "Torture Killer Murders Girl Here, Attempts to Burn Her Body," April 16, 1934.
229. Ibid.
230. Butler, Autopsy Report of Mae Giffin.
231. *Shreveport Times*, "Discovery of Body of Slain Girl is Related," April 17, 1934.
232. *Shreveport Journal*, "Officers Seek Girl's Slayer, Finding of Knife Used In Killing," April 17, 1934.
233. *Shreveport Times*, "Lengthy Hunt for Lockhart Ends Monday," *Shreveport Times*, April 17, 1934.

234. *Shreveport Journal*, April 17, 1934.
235. Ibid.
236. *Shreveport Times*, "Lockhart Confesses Girl Torture Murder," April 18, 1934.
237. *State of Louisiana v. D.B. Napier, alias Fred Lockhart*, 1934; *Shreveport Times*, "Lockhart Confesses Girl Torture Murder," April 18, 1934; *Shreveport Journal*, "Fred Lockhart Confesses that He Killed Girl," April 18, 1934.
238. Brock, *Brock's Shreveport*, 196.
239. *Time*, "Officers Turn Back Frenzied Mob, Troops are Mobilized," April 18, 1934.
240. *Shreveport Journal*, "The Confession," April 18, 1934.
241. *Shreveport Times*, "Authorities Use Tear Gas Effectively," April 18, 1934.
242. Ibid.
243. Ibid.
244. *Shreveport Journal*, "Troops Guard Slayer," April 18, 1934.
245. *Shreveport Journal*, "Grand Jury to Probe Slaying to Meet Friday," April 18, 1934.
246. *Shreveport Journal*, "Lockhart Admits Prison Break: Slayer Confesses he is Fugitive from Georgia Pen," April 19, 1934.
247. *Shreveport Times*, "Lockhart Says he Was Car Driver for Mob Which Hanged Leo Frank," April 20, 1934.
248. *Shreveport Journal*, "Lockhart Was Participant in Leo Frank Case," April 19, 1934.
249. *Shreveport Times*, "Lockhart's Plea of Guilty to Two Crimes Rejected by Judge," April 21, 1934.
250. *Shreveport Journal*, "Prisoner is Quickly Arraigned and Case is Set for Monday," April 20, 1934.
251. *Shreveport Journal*, "Jurors Return Guilty Verdict in Minutes," April 23, 1934.
252. Ibid.
253. Ibid.
254. Ibid.
255. Ibid.
256. *Shreveport Times*, "Lockhart Crime Career Nearing End on Gallows," April 24, 1934.
257. *Shreveport Times*, "Jurors Return Guilty Verdict in Minutes," April 23, 1934.

258. Ibid.
259. *Shreveport Times*, "Lockhart Crime Career Nearing End on Gallows," April 24, 1934.
260. *Shreveport Times*, "Jurors Return Guilty Verdict in Minutes," April 23, 1934.
261. *Shreveport Times*, "Lockhart Crime Career Nearing End on Gallows," April 24, 1934.
262. *Shreveport Times*, "Jurors Return Guilty Verdict in Minutes," April 23, 1934.
263. *Shreveport Times*, "Lockhart Crime Career Nearing End on Gallows," April 24, 1934.
264. State of Louisiana v. D.B. Napier alias Fred Lockhart, 1934.
265. *Shreveport Times*, "Lockhart May be Executed This Weekend," April 25, 1934.
266. *Shreveport Times*, "The Butterfly Man," December 3, 1976.
267. Brock, *Brock's Shreveport*, 196.

Chapter 7

268. Burrough, *Public Enemies*, 16.
269. Milner, *Lives and Times of Bonnie and Clyde*, 3.
270. Theoharis, *The FBI*, 266.
271. Kupperberg, *Critical Perspectives*, 126–27.
272. Theoharis, *The FBI*, 266.
273. Prime, "Infamous Pair Often Reported."
274. Ibid.
275. Milner, *Lives and Times of Bonnie and Clyde*, 6.
276. Treheme, *Strange History of Bonnie and Clyde*, 55–58.
277. Simpson, "Bienville Parish Saga," 9.
278. Guinn, *Go Down Together*, 174.
279. *Shreveport Times*, "Infamous Pair Often Reported in Area," May 17, 2009.
280. Guinn, *Go Down Together*, 181.
281. Simpson, "Bienville Parish Saga," 12.
282. Treheme, *Strange History of Bonnie and Clyde*, 175. (Raymond Hamilton was eventually recaptured and was executed in May 1935.)
283. Simpson, "Bienville Parish Saga," 14.

284. Ibid., 15–16.
285. Hinton, *Ambush*, 168–71.
286. Rich, "Autopsy of Bonnie and Clyde," 33.

Chapter 8

287. Holmes and Holmes, *Serial Murder*, 157.
288. Ibid., 158.
289. Ibid., 218.
290. The figure of five thousand victims per year was brought forward by B. Bernick and J. Spangler in a September 1985 article entitled "Rovers Kill Up to 5,000 Each Year, Experts Say," *Deseret News*, Las Vegas. Quoted in Homes and Homes, *Serial Murder*, 234.
291. Holmes and Holmes, *Serial Murder*, 219.
292. http://www.fbi.gov/about-us/training/bsu.
293. http://www.fbi.gov/about-us/cirg/investigations-and-operations-support. The best single-volume work in this field is found in Douglas and Olshaker, *Mind Hunter*.
294. John E. Douglas is the author, coauthor or editor of fifteen books. His career served as the basis for the Jack Crawford character in the Thomas Harris's *Red Dragon* and *Silence of the Lambs* and the Jason Gideon character in CBS television network's *Criminal Minds*. Although retired from the bureau at the time of this writing, Douglas is still active in the field. For more on Jon Douglas, see http://www.johndouglasmindhunter.com/bio.php.
295. *Shreveport Times*, September 1, 1984.
296. Caddo Parish Evidence Room items; *Shreveport Times*, November 15, 2009.
297. Keppel and Birnes, *Signature Killers*, 156–57.
298. Douglas and Munn, "Violent Crime Scene Analysis," 1–10.
299. Former assistant district attorney, now district judge, Scott Crichton, quoted in *Shreveport Times*, November 15, 2009; *Shreveport Times*, September 1, 1984.
300. Dr. George McCormick was the second-longest-serving coroner in the history of Caddo Parish, in office from 1982 until his death in 2005. He was both a medical doctor and a board certified forensic pathologist. Gates, *Shreveport and Caddo Parish Officials*, i49–i52.

301. Bath, http://www.timetoast.com/timelines/26746. Bath is a reporter for the *Shreveport Times*.
302. Louisiana State Penitentiary records.
303. *Shreveport Times*, July 20, 1985; *Shreveport Journal Magazine*, February 14, 1986.
304. Keppel and Birnes, *Signature Killers*, 163-7.
305. *Shreveport Times*, July 20, 1985.
306. Ibid., August 7, 1987.
307. Ramsland, *Forensic Psychology of Criminal Minds*, 108–09.
308. Transcript of John E. Douglas, *State of Louisiana v. Nathaniel Code*; Douglas and Douglas, "Modus Operandi," 19–20.
309. Caddo Parish District Court records.
310. http://www.judgescottcrichton.com/nathanial_code.
311. "Hunting Humans."
312. Ibid.
313. http://www.clarkprosecutor.org/html/death/US/rolling1051.htm. Information in this paragraph serves only as a brief sketch of Rolling's early life and his career as a criminal.
314. Ibid.; "Hunting Humans."
315. *Shreveport Times*, January 25, 1991.
316. Death row diary of Danny Harold Rolling, copy in the records of the Caddo Parish District Attorney, Shreveport, Louisiana.
317. *Shreveport Times*, November 6, 1989.
318. Ibid.
319. Death row diary of Danny Harold Rolling.
320. *Shreveport Journal*, November 7, 1989.
321. *News-Star* [Monroe, Louisiana], November 8, 1989.
322. *Shreveport Times*, November 8, 1989.
323. Narrative Supplement, Shreveport, Louisiana Police Department, January 23, 1990.
324. Ibid.
325. Ibid.
326 *Shreveport Journal*, November 11, 1989; *Shreveport Times*, November 18, 1989; November 9, 1990; November 11, 1995; Whitehead, "Hal Carter," 10–17.
327. *Shreveport Journal*, January 26, 2991.
328. http://www.clarkprosecutor.org/html/death/US/rolling1051.htm.
329. *Shreveport Times*, October 17, 1990.

330. *Shreveport Journal*, October 18, 1990.
331. Death row diary of Danny Harold Rolling.
332. http://www.clarkprosecutor.org/html/death/US/rolling1051.htm.
333. Homes and Holmes, *Serial Murder*, 104.
334. See particularly Douglas and Olshaker, *Mind Hunter*; Douglas and Olshaker, *Anatomy of Motive*; Douglas and Olshaker, *Cases That Haunt Us*; and Douglas and Olshaker, *Journey Into Darkness*.

Bibliography

Manuscripts

Albert Harris Leonard Memoirs. Archives and Special Collections, Noel Memorial Library, Louisiana State University in Shreveport.
Alfred Flournoy Sr. Family Papers, Archives and Special Collections, Noel Memorial Library, Louisiana State University in Shreveport.
B'nai Zion Cemetery Records
Foster Family Papers. Archives and Special Collections, Noel Memorial Library, Louisiana State University in Shreveport.
John Gray Foster Memorial Volume. Collection of Mary T. McGuire, Shreveport, Louisiana.
Slattery Family Papers. Collection of Joseph Slattery, Shreveport, Louisiana.

Books and Articles

Alexander, Charles C. *The Ku Klux Klan in the Southwest.* Lexington: University of Kentucky Press, 1965.
Brock, Eric. *Eric Brock's Shreveport.* Gretna, LA: Pelican Publishing Company, 2001.
Brundage, W. Fitzhugh. *Lynching in the New South: Georgia and Virginia, 1880–1930.* Urbana: University of Illinois Press, 1993.

———. *Under Sentence of Death: Lynching in the South*. Chapel Hill: University of North Carolina Press, 1997.

Burrough, Bryan. *Public Enemies: America's Greatest Crime Wave and the Birth of the FBI, 1933–34*. New York: Penguin Books, 2004.

Clark, Norman H. *Deliver Us from Evil: An Interpretation of American Prohibition*. New York: W.W. Norton & Company, Inc., 1976.

Coffey, Thomas M. *The Long Thirst: Prohibition in America: 1920–1933*. New York: W.W. Norton & Company, Inc., 1975.

Dauphine, James G. "The Knights of the White Camellia and the Election of 1868: Louisiana's White Terrorists; A Benighting Legacy." *Louisiana History: The Journal of the Louisiana Historical Association* 30, no. 2 (Spring 1989): 173–90.

Ditmore, Melissa H. *Encyclopedia of Prostitution and Sex Work*. Westport, CT: Greenwood Press, 2006.

Douglas, John E., and Corrine Munn. "Violent Crime Scene Analysis: Modus Operandi, Signature, and Staging," in *FBI Law Enforcement Bulletin*, February 1992, 1-10.

Douglas, John E., and Lauren K. Douglas. "Modus Operandi and the Signature Aspects of Violent Crime." In *Crime Classification Manual: A Standard System for Investigating and Classifying Violent Crimes*. San Francisco, CA, 2006.

Douglas, John E. and Mark Olshaker. *Mind Hunter: Inside the FBI's Elite Serial Crime Unit*. New York: Pocket Books, 1996.

Drago, Harry Sinclair. *The Great Range Wars: Violence on the Grasslands*. Lincoln: University of Nebraska Press, 1985.

Du Bois, W.E.B. *Black Reconstruction in America, 1860–1880*. New York: Harcourt, Brace, 1935.

Esselstyn, T.C. "Prostitution in the United States." *Annals of the American Academy of Political and Social Science* 376 (March 1968).

Gates, Carol. *Shreveport and Caddo Parish Officials: 1836–1986*. Shreveport, LA: Shreve Memorial Library, 1986.

Ginzburg, Ralph. *100 Years of Lynchings*. Baltimore, MD: Black Classic Press, 1988.

Guinn, Jeff. *Go Down Together: The True, Untold Story of Bonnie and Clyde*. New York: Simon and Schuster, 2009.

Harrell, K. "The Ku Klux Klan in Louisiana, 1920–1930." PhD diss., Louisiana State University, 1966.

Bibliography

Hennick, Louis C., and E. Harper Charlton. *Louisiana: Its Street and Interurban Railways.* Shreveport, LA: Journal Printing Co., 1962.

Henrice, Holice. *Shreveport, the Beginnings.* Lafayette: Center for Louisiana Studies, 1985.

Hinton, Ted. *Ambush: The Real Story of Bonnie and Clyde.* Austin, TX: Shoal Creek Publishers, 1979.

Hogue, James K. *Uncivil War: Five New Orleans Street Battles and the Rise and Fall of Radical Reconstruction.* Baton Rouge: Louisiana State University Press, 2006.

Holmes, Ronald M., and Stephen T. Holmes. *Serial Murder.* Thousand Oaks, CA: Sage Publications, 2010.

Jackson, Joy. "Prohibition in New Orleans: The Unlikeliest Crusade." *Louisiana History: The Journal of the Louisiana Historical Association* 19, no. 3 (Summer 1978): 261–84.

Joiner, Gary D., and Ernie Roberson. *Lost Shreveport: Vanishing Scenes from the Red River Valley.* Charleston, SC, 2010.

Keire, Mara L. *For Business and Pleasure: Red-Light Districts and the Regulation of Vice in the United States, 1890–1933.* Baltimore, MD: Johns Hopkins University Press, 2010.

Keppel, Robert D., and William J. Birnes. *Signature Killers: Interpreting the Calling Cards of Serial Killers.* New York: Pocket Books, 1997.

King, William Henry. *No Pardons to Ask, nor Apologies to Make: The Journal of William Henry King, Gray's 28th Louisiana Infantry Regiment.* Edited by Gary D. Joiner, Marilyn S. Joiner and Clifton D. Cardin. Knoxville: University of Tennessee Press, 2006.

Kupperberg, Paul. *Critical Perspectives on the Great Depression.* New York: Rosen Publishing Group, 2005.

Kyvig, David E. *Repealing National Prohibition.* Chicago: University of Chicago Press, 1979

Lornell, Kip, and Tracey Laird. *Shreveport Sounds in Black and White.* University Press of Mississippi. 2008.

McLure, Lila, and J. Ed Howe. *History of Shreveport and Shreveport Builders.* Shreveport, LA: J. Ed Howe Publisher, 1937.

Milner, E.R. *The Lives and Times of Bonnie and Clyde.* Carbondale: Southern Illinois University Press, 1996.

O'Pry, Maude Hearn. *Chronicles of Shreveport.* Shreveport, LA: Journal Printing Co., 1927.

Peoples, Morgan D. "'Kansas Fever' in North Louisiana." *Louisiana History: The Journal of the Louisiana Historical Association* 11, no. 2 (Spring 1970): 121–35.
Perman, Michael. *Pursuit of Unity: A Political History of the American South.* Chapel Hill: University of North Carolina Press, 2009.
Pfeiffer, Michael J. "Lynching and Criminal Justice in South Louisiana, 1878–1930," *Louisiana History* 40, no. 2 (Spring 1999): 155–77.
———. *Rough Justice: Lynching and American Society, 1874–1947.* Urbana: University of Illinois Press, 2004.
Ramsland, Katherine. *The Forensic Psychology of Criminal Minds.* New York: Berkley, 2010.
Randel, William Peirce. *The Ku Klux Klan: A Century of Infamy.* Philadelphia: Chilton Books, 1965.
Raper, Arthur F. *The Tragedy of Lynching.* Chapel Hill: University of North Carolina Press, 1933.
Rich, Carroll Y. "The Autopsy of Bonnie and Clyde." *Western Folklore* 29, no. 1 (January 1970).
Ruffin, Tom. "The Invasion of Shreveport." *Shreveport Magazine*, July 1969.
Sanger, William. *History of Prostitution: Its Extents, Causes and Effects Throughout the World.* New York: Harper and Row, 1858.
Schultz, Duane. *Quantrill's War: The Life and Times of William Clarke Quantrill, 1837–1865.* New York: Macmillan, 1997.
Simpson, William. "A Bienville Parish Saga: The Ambush and Killing of Bonnie and Clyde." *Louisiana History: The Journal of the Louisiana Historical Association* 41, no. 1 (Winter 2000).
Stelzle, Charles. *Why Prohibition!* New York: George H. Doran Co., 1918.
Stuck, Goodloe. *Annie McCune: Shreveport Madam.* Baton Rouge, LA: Moran Publishing Company, 1981.
Taylor, Joe Gray. *Louisiana Reconstructed, 1863–1877.* Baton Rouge: Louisiana State University Press, 1974.
Theoharis, Athan. *The FBI: A Comprehensive Reference Guide.* Phoenix, AZ: Oryx Press, 1999.
Tolnay, Stewart E., and E.M. Beck. *A Festival of Violence: An Analysis of Southern Lynchings, 1882–1930.* Urbana: University of Illinois Press, 1995.
Tracey, E.W., and Kip Lornell. *Shreveport Sounds in Black and White.* Jackson: University of Mississippi Press, 2008.
Treheme, John E. *Strange History of Bonnie and Clyde.* New York: Cooper Square Press, 2000.

Trelease, Allen W. *White Terror: The Ku Klux Klan Conspiracy and Southern Reconstruction.* Baton Rouge: Louisiana State University Press, 1971.

Tunnell, Ted. *Crucible of Reconstruction: War, Radicalism and Race in Louisiana, 1862–1877.* Baton Rouge: Louisiana State University Press, 1984.

———. *Edge of the Sword: The Ordeal of Carpetbagger Marshall H. Twitchell in the Civil War and Reconstruction.* Baton Rouge: Louisiana State University Press, 2001.

Vance, Robert Patrick. "The Demise of Prohibition." *The Concord Review* (2001): 97–116.

Vandal, Gilles. "Albert H. Leonard's Road from the White League to the Republican Party: A Political Enigma." *Louisiana History: The Journal of the Louisiana Historical Association* 36, no. 1 (Winter 1995): 55–76.

———. "'Bloody Caddo': White Violence Against Blacks in a Louisiana Parish, 1865–1876." *Journal of Social History* 25, no. 2 (Winter 1991): 373–88.

———. "The Policy of Violence in Caddo Parish, 1865–1884." *Louisiana History: The Journal of the Louisiana Historical Association* 32, no. 2 (Spring 1991): 159–82.

———. *Rethinking Southern Violence: Homicides in Post-Civil War Louisiana, 1866–1884.* Columbus: Ohio State University Press, 2000.

Wade, Wyn Craig. *The Fiery Cross: The Ku Klux Klan in America.* New York: Simon & Schuster, Inc., 1987.

Walker, Samuel. *Popular Justice: A History of American Criminal Justice.* New York: Oxford University Press, 1980.

Whitehead, Mike. "Hal Carter: Judge Not: The True Story of Murder, Madness and Vindication," *SB Magazine*, May 2007.

Woolston, Howard B. *Prostitution in the United States.* Vol. I. New York: Century Company, 1921.

Government Documents

Butler, Willis, MD. Autopsy Report of Mae Giffin, Office of the Coroner of Caddo Parish, April 15, 1934.

Caddo Parish (Louisiana) District Attorney's Records. Death Row diary of Danny Harold Rolling.

Caddo Parish (Louisiana) Evidence Room, Caddo District Court.

Caddo Parish (Louisiana) Records. Probate Record of James Martin Foster Sr. Caddo Parish Clerk of Court Record Book 26, page 341, files, December 18, 1900.

BIBLIOGRAPHY

Caddo Parish (Louisiana) Records. Succession of S.C. Willson, Probate No. 43 (1841). Caddo Parish Clerk of Court.

Douglas, John E. Transcript, *State of Louisiana v. Nathaniel Code*. First Judicial District Court in and for the Parish of Caddo, Shreveport, Louisiana. Case No. 138, 860, July 21, 1989.

Extremism and Radicalization Branch, Homeland Environment Threat Analysis Division. *Rightwing Extremism: Current Economic and Political Climate Fueling Resurgence in Radicalization and Recruitment.* IA-0257-09. Washington, D.C.: Office of Intelligence and Analysis, 2009.

Louisiana General Assembly. *Report of Joint Committee of the General Assembly of Louisiana on the Conduct of the Late Elections and the Condition of Peace and Order in the State.* Session of 1869. New Orleans, 1869.

Louisiana State Penitentiary Records, Angola, Louisiana.

Senate Documents. *Reports of Committees of the Senate of the United States for the First and Second Sessions of the Forty-Sixth Congress, 1879–80. Exodus Committee*, "Negro Exodus From Southern States." Washington, D.C. : Government Printing Office, 1880.

Shreveport City Records. Proceedings of the City Council of Shreveport, Louisiana. Louisiana State University at Shreveport Archives and Special Collections, Collection 453.

Shreveport Police Department. Narrative Supplement. Profile by the Federal Bureau of Investigation, Behavioral Science Unit, January 23, 1990.

State of Louisiana v. D.B. Napier, alias Fred Lockhart. 1934.

State of Louisiana v. Gus Logan. No. 6214.

Supreme Court, State of Louisiana v. Gus Logan. 37 LA Ann. 778, No. 165.

U.S. Dept. of Commerce. Seventh Decennial Census (1850), Caddo Parish, Louisiana. Unpublished tabulations in the National Archives and Records Administration, Washington, D.C.

———. Twelfth Decennial Census (1900), Caddo Parish, Louisiana. Census Place: Shreveport Ward 1, Caddo, Louisiana; Roll T623_560; Page: 1B; Enumeration District: 39. Unpublished tabulations in the National Archives and Records Administration, Washington, D.C.

U.S. Congress. *Report of the Joint Select Committee to Inquire into the Condition of Affairs in the Late Insurrectionary States Made to the Two Houses of Congress, February 19, 1872* Washington, D.C.: Government Printing Office, 1872.

Bibliography

Websites

Anti-Defamation League. "Ku Klux Klan: Extremism in America." http://www.adl.org/learn/ext_us/kkk/history.asp?LEARN_Cat=Extremism&LEARN_SubCat=Extremism_in_America&xpicked=4&item=kkk.

Bath, Alison. "Code Timeline." http://www.timetoast.com/timelines/26746.

Clark County (Florida) Prosecutors' Office. http://www.clarkprosecutor.org/html/death/US/rolling1051.htm.

Crichton, Scott. http://www.judgescottcrichton.com/nathanial_code.

Douglas, John E. http://www.johndouglasmindhunter.com/bio.php.

Federal Bureau of Investigation. http://www.fbi.gov/about-us/training/bsu.

———. http://www.fbi.gov/about-us/cirg/investigations-and-operations-support.

Oakland Cemetery Preservation Society. http://www.oaklandcemeteryla.org/Index.aspx.

Southern Poverty Law Center. "Hate Map." http://www.splcenter.org/get-informed/hate-map.

Digital Media

"Hunting Humans: Rolling, Danny Harold." *Mind of a Killer*. CD-ROM, Wadsworth Thomson Learning, 1995.

Newspapers

Alexandria [Louisiana] *Caucasian*, April 4, 1874.
Aurora [Illinois] *Daily Express*, June 14, 1901.
Chicago Record-Herald, June 20, 1901; July 27, 1903.
Columbus [Georgia] *Daily Enquirer*, June 15, 1901; June 21, 1901.
Desert News [Las Vegas, Nevada], September 1985.
Dallas Morning News, June 13, 1901; January 14, 1910.
Montgomery [Alabama] *Advertiser*, April 10, 1912; April 26, 1959.

BIBLIOGRAPHY

New Orleans Item, June 15, 1901; June 21, 1901; December 17, 1909.
News-Star [Monroe, Louisiana], November 8, 1989.
New York Times, June 18, 1885; June 13, 1901; June 14, 1901.
Omaha [Nebraska] *World Herald*, June 20, 1901.
Philadelphia Enquirer, August 27, 1916.
Shreveport Journal, June 15, 1901; August 26, 1916; September 15, 1923; April 17, 1934; April 18, 1934; April 19, 1934; April 20, 1934; April 10, 1971; November 7, 1989; November 8, 1989; November 11, 1989; October 18, 1990; January 26, 1991;
Shreveport Journal Magazine, February 14, 1986.
Shreveport Times, October 1, 1873; November 15, 1873; July 9, 1874; November 29, 1892; June 15, 1901; July 26, 1903; November 28, 1909; January 14, 1910; April 9, 1912; August 26, 1916; January 4, 1923; April 16, 1934; April 17, 1934; April 18, 1934; April 19, 1934; April 20, 1934; 21, 1934; April 23, 1934; April 24, 1934; April 25, 1934. December 3, 1976; September 1, 1984; July 20, 1985; August 7, 1987; November 6, 1989; November 18, 1989; October 17, 1990; November 9, 1990; January 25, 1991; November 11, 1995; May 17, 2009; May 18, 2009; November 15, 2009.
Times-Picayune [New Orleans] December 13, 1900; January 1, 1908; January 15, 1908; October 3, 1909; June 17, 1910; January 31, 1911; October 22, 1911; July 8, 1912; February 10, 1913; March 4, 1913; April 3, 1913; July 4, 1913; June 30, 1915; October 18, 1915; December 20, 1915; April 7, 1916; October 9, 1916; December 9, 1917; August 9, 1918; January 6, 1919; January 16, 1920.

About the Authors

BERNADETTE J. PALOMBO is a professor of criminal justice and chair of the Department of History and Social Sciences at Louisiana State University in Shreveport. She holds a doctorate in political science and a master's degree in criminal justice from the Center for Politics and Economics at the Claremont Graduate University, Claremont, California. She is a member of Alpha Phi Sigma National Criminal Justice Honor Society, the Academy of Criminal Justice Sciences and the American Society of Criminology.

GARY D. JOINER is the Mary Anne and Leonard Selber Professor of History at Louisiana State University in Shreveport, where he teaches both history and geography and serves as director of the Red River Regional Studies Center. He holds a bachelor's degree in history and geography and a master's degree in history from Louisiana Tech University and earned his PhD in history from St. Martin's College, Lancaster University, in the United Kingdom. Dr. Joiner is past president of the North Louisiana Civil War Round Table and the DeSoto Historical Society and is president and founder of the Friends of the Mansfield Battlefield. History is both his profession and his hobby. In 2010, he was named Preservationist of the Year by the Louisiana Trust for Historic Preservation. He is series editor for Western Theater in the Civil War with the University of Tennessee Press. He writes the "History Doctor" column for *Forum News* and presents a weekly "History Matters" commentary on Red River Radio, public radio.

About the Authors

W. CHRIS HALE is an assistant professor of criminal justice at Louisiana State University in Shreveport. He has published and presented research in the areas of cybercrime, terrorism and intelligence analysis. Most recently, he has had his work published in the *Proteus Futures Digest* and the *International Journal of Emergency Management*. He is a member of several professional organizations, including the American Society of Criminology and the Academy of Criminal Justice Sciences. Currently, Dr. Hale is working on research concerning extremist use of the Internet.

CHERYL H. WHITE is the Hubert Humphreys Professor of History at Louisiana State University in Shreveport. She has published extensively in the field of medieval and Reformation history, as well as local history. Most recently, she coauthored another History Press title with Gary Joiner, *Historic Haunts of Shreveport*, and is a regular contributor to local and regional publications on historical topics. Dr. White is also a frequent regional and national speaker and has won numerous teaching awards.

www.ingramcontent.com/pod-product-compliance
Lightning Source LLC
Chambersburg PA
CBHW042144160426
43201CB00022B/2401